BREAKING

THE

CIRCUIT

BREAKING
THE
CIRCUIT

How to Rewire Your Mind for Hope,
Resilience, and Joy in the Face of Trauma

DR. SAMANTHA HARTE

GREENLEAF
BOOK GROUP PRESS

This book is intended as a reference volume only. It is sold with the understanding that the publisher and author are not engaged in rendering any professional services. The information given here is designed to help you make informed decisions. If you suspect that you have a problem that might require professional treatment or advice, you should seek competent help.

Published by Greenleaf Book Group Press
Austin, Texas
www.gbgpress.com

Copyright © 2024 Dr. Samantha Harte

Distributed by Greenleaf Book Group

For ordering information or special discounts for bulk purchases, please contact Greenleaf Book Group at PO Box 91869, Austin, TX 78709, 512.891.6100.

Design and composition by Greenleaf Book Group and Sheila Parr
Cover design by Greenleaf Book Group and Sheila Parr
Cover images © Shutterstock/cybermagician and Shutterstock/wawritto

Publisher's Cataloging-in-Publication data is available.

Print ISBN: 979-8-88645-196-2

eBook ISBN: 979-8-88645-197-9

To offset the number of trees consumed in the printing of our books, Greenleaf donates a portion of the proceeds from each printing to the Arbor Day Foundation. Greenleaf Book Group has replaced over 50,000 trees since 2007.

Printed in the United States of America on acid-free paper
24 25 26 27 28 29 30 31   10 9 8 7 6 5 4 3 2 1
First Edition

To Jack and Charly:

May you always look for the light in the darkest tunnel.
May you always remember your worthiness in the greatest
mistakes. May you always know you have the power to
break the cycle of dysfunction.

CONTENTS

INTRODUCTION

ONCE UPON A TIME, JUST after her acceptance to a prestigious doctoral program, a young woman overdosed on cocaine. She survived, waking up to a look of horror in her friend's eyes, a clear indicator that something awful had happened. Vowing never to do cocaine again, she kept up pretenses, studying hard during the day and playing harder in the New York City club scene at night. To the outside world, she had her shit together—the job, the body, the boyfriend—but somewhere deep inside, she knew this would all come crashing down sooner or later. That woman was me.

But that's not even the interesting part of the story. This near-death experience didn't hold a candle to the spiritual bottom I would hit years later as my marriage unraveled and I lost many people I loved. The real story is the one about the gift of desperation—that sacred place where seemingly all has been lost, where every wiring pattern I relied on as a kid and exhausted into adulthood stopped working. In this place, desperation meets willingness and creates a holy space where "God" becomes an idea born from you, not imposed on you. The real story begins at the emotional and physical edge, where the nervous system and the soul are primed for a new experience. This is the place where the foundation cracks—a place where the light seeps in.

I'm not sure about you, but I have an iron will. For me, as a hardwired perfectionist, the difficulty in "letting go" or "trusting the process" is twofold. First, my real drug of choice is control. I have an insatiable appetite for a neat and orderly world. Second, the neurological patterns for maintaining control at all costs have been deeply ingrained in me since childhood because I relied on them to stay alive.

Growing up around addiction, enablement, infidelity, and mental illness meant that I got extremely good at taking the emotional temperature of the room and changing my insides to match the outside. The motto I operated from boils down to this: *If I love you hard enough, maybe you won't leave me.* One neural pathway at a time, my nervous system became trained in how to please others and abandon myself, distrust my inner knowing, and give my love away until there was nothing left of me.

When you couple this with the deeply conditioned messaging of Western culture where control and perfectionism generate high praise, you've got yourself a recipe for disaster. I wholeheartedly bought into ideas like, *The more you do and the more you have, the better. The more degrees, promotions, properties, prestige, and praise you accumulate, the happier you will be. All you have to do is follow some basic guidelines, and the life of your dreams is right over there.*

But what my childhood and culture didn't teach is that perfectionism collapses in matters of the heart. There is no such thing as a clear path through betrayal, forgiveness, or grief. And even when you survive them and rediscover joy, you will always be holding hands with two opposing dichotomies at once—love and loss, forgiveness and resentment, hope and despair. Whether we like it or not, that's what it means to be fully alive. Not once have I been able to follow a linear path through disappointment, heartbreak, betrayal, or addiction—and boy, did I try.

I am fifteen years sober from drugs and alcohol, which is the best, hardest, and most courageous thing I have ever done. That said, the more time I accumulate sober, the more I realize that the Twelve Steps of Alcoholics Anonymous—yes, the ones found in addiction recovery rooms—are universally applicable to personal transformation no matter who you are.

When I first heard the Twelve Steps, I hated them on a visceral level. They sounded religious, archaic, and utterly irrelevant to my drinking and drugging problem. So I tried to live the way I had always lived—obsessively controlling the people, places, and things around me to feel safe. Things kept falling apart. No matter how intelligent or adamant I was, I found that the tighter I held on to my old ideas, the more quickly things fell through my hands.

Eventually, my emotional despair became so great that I turned to the Steps, but I reimagined them so that they worked for me and not against me. The Twelve Steps are the same in every program about addiction—whether the dependency involves food, money, sex, drugs, or relationships. "Addiction, which has been viewed historically as a 'moral deficiency,' is being increasingly regarded as a chronic relapsing disorder characterized by an urge to consume drugs and by the progressive loss of control over, and escalation in, drug intake despite repeated (unsuccessful) attempts to resist doing it."[1] I started to wonder what would happen if we understood the why behind it all; if we stopped focusing on the symptoms of the addict—compulsive behavior, erratic decisions, self-sabotaging thoughts—and got down to the root causes. If I learned to become highly vigilant as a child to feel safe, and now as an adult I numb my feelings when I feel unstable, can I learn how to feel secure in a healthy way? Can I practice new behaviors that rewire my old coping patterns? Can the Twelve Steps give me a blueprint for living a spiritual life in a way that resonates with me?

I reconstructed what it meant to be powerless, accountable, and faithful in the face of perfectionism, martyrdom, and

---

1 Nora D. Volkow, Michael Michaelides, and Ruben Baler, "The Neuroscience of Drug Reward and Addiction," *Physiological Reviews* 99 (2019), https://journals.physiology.org/doi/full/10.1152/physrev.00014.2018.

self-reliance. Over many months, my old wiring patterns weakened as I practiced new ones. Instead of manhandling my life, I learned to live in the unknown spaces and cultivate trust around outcomes I couldn't see.

At first, I did this because I had to. But eventually, I realized that I was operating from a place of survival, a nervous system that was highly overactive and ready to protect me at all costs—even at the expense of my sanity. With some time in recovery, the Twelve Steps gave me access to a new peace and a new freedom. I discovered that if I sat through the unknown, faith would trickle in. If I held hands with my suffering, joy would find me. If I interrogated my anger, forgiveness would appear.

In 2010, I was barely two years sober and graduated with a doctorate in physical therapy. I knew only a few things for sure. First, I wanted to help people. Second, if I drank again, I would die. My career began like many others. I took a job in a typical outpatient setting and hoped to help people recover. I quickly realized the health-care landscape set patients up to fail, covering a handful of visits and then discharging them well before they were recovered. I decided to open my own practice in Santa Monica, California, with the goal to bridge the gap between patient dismissal and the level of recovery they longed for. I am proud to say I helped a lot of people because I valued becoming a good clinician above money and prestige. I treated whole people and became a practitioner who listened, learned, and cared. I pieced together the symptom presentation until I got to the source. Clients who found me were the ones who had tried everything and failed. They showed up at my doorstep with willingness and a healthy dose of despair.

However, after many years of thoroughly assessing bodies and carefully designing programs, I realized there was still a gaping hole between what I was offering and my patients' ability to get well. Yes, they made a mental commitment to stop doing the things that led to pain, but their head and heart were not yet integrated.

Emotionally, they were still stuck in a pattern that would inhibit their full recovery.

"Did you practice the exercises?" I'd ask. "Well, I was going to, but I got stuck on a damn call with the lawyer again and it was time for bed before I knew it," they'd say. Or "I was all ready to work out and then my kid got upset. My husband didn't know how to deal with him, so I had to." One after another I listened as people described what I have come to call "soul sickness," which has a consistent pattern despite differing circumstances—we repeat patterns and behaviors we once needed (often subconsciously) that are now harmful to us, and they stand in the way of the bodies, relationships, and lives we really want.

I realized that no matter how good of a practitioner I was or how sophisticated a program I designed, I couldn't cure people's addiction to productivity, martyrdom, or quick fixes. I couldn't fix the deep core belief that success means grind until you collapse or love means abandon yourself until you disappear. I realized these ordinary people, much like the addicts I had come to know and love in recovery, were suffering from something much greater than knee pain. They were in a cycle of spiritual dysfunction, and their recovery was contingent on a level of readiness that was not just physical. I could spend days and weeks rewiring their nervous system through scientific and progressive exercise, but they had to simultaneously be ready and willing to rewire their emotional nervous system. Otherwise, the house of cards would eventually crumble.

Most of my patients were not addicts. But our journeys, struggles, and desires were not so different. Mind-body connection is, at its deepest level, the integration of our intellect and spirit so we can live in a way that is aligned with our values and integrity. It is excavating our secrets, triggers, and unhealthy behaviors and meeting them with compassion and consistency. Making micro-changes that lead to macro-results. This is the kind of work that shifts pain into power.

I've navigated betrayal and grief in enormous quantities throughout my life. In most cases, my reaction to crisis begins with a fierce reaction to control, fix, change, or numb the situation. Then, when that inevitably fails, I hit a spiritual bottom and become willing to try something new. From that place, I practice new behaviors, sometimes ones that challenge every coping mechanism I know, and eventually I have a new experience. Slowly, over time, my nervous system creates new feedback loops for how to handle things like heartbreak, infidelity, insanity, and death. What I find again and again is that hope, joy, laughter, and play are always there waiting. Sometimes it feels impossible, I know. But we are either walking through life half dead or fully alive. What's your choice?

This book takes you on a journey. Through the stories of my life, I explain how, against all odds, I turned trauma into triumph. I describe the science behind the lengths that the body will go to hold on to what it knows, as well as its ability to be reprogrammed no matter what it has been through. As you learn about my life, you will see the odds were stacked pretty high against me. I easily could have ended up on skid row with a needle in my arm; I easily could have ended up dead.

Was some luck involved in getting me where I am today? Absolutely. Mostly, though, I worked very hard at changing the trajectory of my life. At each emotional bottom, I discovered a willingness to try something new. I held myself. I asked for help. I apologized. I told the truth. I slowed down. I did things that at one point seemed unimaginable until they became intrinsic, woven into the fabric of who I am today. My emotional well-being became contingent at any given time on how often I was using the Twelve Steps to navigate the precise life situation I was in. It has been my experience again and again that the Steps can be used for anything, big or small, to access more clarity, compassion, freedom, and joy. And if I do nothing else right on this earth, I at least want to share it with you.

I've found the more I use the Twelve Steps to navigate the business of everyday living, whether it's the condescending boss, the toxic relationship, or the goddamn traffic, the more passionately I believe they can work for everyone. Addict or not, all of us suffer from some degree of soul sickness. We humans navigate love and loss throughout the lifespan with little to no guidance, often fumbling our way through with self-sabotaging behaviors we adopted in childhood or numbing practices our culture spoon-feeds us.

Breaking the Circuit is a book for the people who have tried everything and failed, on a soul level, to navigate life's hardest things. My goal for this book is to make the language of the Twelve Steps current so their underlying messages are accessible for as many people as possible. After fifteen years sober, I have found that they are less about physical sobriety and more about emotional sobriety; they are a guide for how to stay open, honest, and hopeful through some of life's toughest situations. Each chapter correlates with one of the Twelve Steps and extracts the universal message to help you, the reader, see how transformative the work can be when we practice a little bit at a time.

I've watched so many people I love, including myself, emotionally shut down in the face of pain. And when they armor up, one of two things happens. They either die a slow, spiritual death, spending their lives walking among the living lonely, disconnected, angry, and afraid; or they die a tragic physical death because the pain of living was too great. I am here to tell you there is a way out of this dichotomy, and it is available to everyone—to you—regardless of where you come from or what you've been through.

Welcome, and I hope you stay.

1

MY MAMA
TAUGHT ME THAT

ALL JOURNEYS START WITH THE first step, and personal transformation is no different. So let's talk about Step One:

> We admitted we were powerless over alcohol—
> that our lives had become unmanageable.[2]

Step One, in the context of addiction, is both brutal and critical. Brutal because admitting we have lost complete control over something that we feel we need to literally survive is gut-wrenching. Critical because if we do not admit absolute defeat, we will drink again, and to drink is to die, whether it's a slow, spiritual death or a sudden, physical one.

There is a saying in recovery that the only step you must do perfectly is Step One. Why? Because if you think you have power over your substance of choice, then picking up a drink or a drug

---

2   Alcoholics Anonymous World Services, *Twelve Steps and Twelve Traditions* (New York: Alcoholics Anonymous World Services, 1981), 21.

will become a logical decision. And then, if you truly suffer from addiction, all bets are off. Even if you refuse the rest of the Steps and bulldoze your way through life, you will at least stay physically (not emotionally) sober.

But what is admitting powerlessness and unmanageability to the "ordinary" person who is not an addict? What does that mean and why does it matter? Whether we realize it or not, we are faced with examples of powerlessness every day. We don't know if we got the job. We don't know if we'll hit traffic. We don't know if our friendship will last. We don't know if that thing we just said will damage our child forever. We are all faced with tons of situations we are powerless over, so what do we do?

We can obsessively check our emails to see if we got the job offer, time our commute perfectly to avoid traffic, manipulate our words to control what people think of us, and redirect our children's emotions through bribery, distraction, or discipline. We can spend the entire day exerting control over things we honestly have *no* control over, which not only results in stress and a dysregulated nervous system but is also the equivalent to running in place when you're trying to make the train. We can try and exert power over all kinds of things, but this strategy leads to exhaustion. You might feel angry, resentful, and anxious. You might consider your life unmanageable. Does this sound familiar?

What if I told you there was another way. What if the idea of power was redirected inward—what do you have actual power over? Not the weather, not the traffic, not the pollution or the politics or the wars. Not the job, not the bad date you went on, and not the dog's accident in the middle of the night. What you *do* have power over is how you show up to these life situations. How do you respond? How do you take action? How do you speak to yourself? At what point (if any) do you surrender?

This is a lot harder than it sounds, particularly if you're type A, like me. When perfectionism is paired with the cultural conditioning that certain steps lead to specific outcomes, we are set up for failure. We often believe deep in our bones that we can solve our own problems with our own manpower. And until we try this again and again without success, we will keep doing what we've always done.

WHAT I LEARNED ABOUT POWER FROM MY MAMA

Before I got sober, I spent my life trying to control the world around me and the people in it. I am a hardwired perfectionist, and when you couple that with an addict's disposition and a very dysfunctional childhood, you become the most culturally productive and spiritually bankrupt human on earth. After years of self-examination, I now know that my desire to control everyone and everything came from a place of great need. Everywhere I looked I saw chaos and confusion, and as a small girl, that was terrifying. Since the most important thing to my own survival was safety, I looked for it every chance I could, often in the form of a question.

"Why do you take those pills every night?" I asked my mother one evening, afraid of her response but resigned to know the answer. Her name was Madison but everyone called her Maddy. Such a friendly name for such a dark soul.

We were standing in the kitchen together as she rummaged through her purse for her meds. She paused and cocked her head to the side, narrowing her eyes.

"Do you like the things you have, Sam?"

I looked down at my blankie and at my favorite stegosaurus toy sitting on the counter nearby and nodded my six-year-old head.

"Well, in order to give you those things, Mommy has to make money," she said, leaning in close so I could see the intensity in her hazel eyes. "And in order for Mommy to make money, she has to work. And in order for Mommy to work, she has to sleep. These pills help me sleep."

I remember feeling confused, but I knew from her tone that I could never ask about it again. My mother is not a saint, but when I was growing up, she was a kind of deity to me. Every word out of her mouth seemed holy, landing in a sacred place in my nervous system, as our mothers' words do.

I don't remember the first time she told me that my dad was a monster; I just remember that I believed her. Not the kind of monster who abuses his loved ones—the kind who emotionally disappears, physically rejects, and carelessly gambles the family's life savings away.

As I grew up, my dad, Benny, was the enabler, taking on the role of family drug dealer to show his affection for his most important people—first with my mom, and later with my sister and me. It started off innocently enough. When my mother would run out of her prescription medication, my father would get the same drugs (which he didn't need) in his name and give them to her, deeply rooting their codependency. Even as a child, I noticed my mother was kind to him when she needed something, but when those needs weren't met, all hell broke loose: screaming, cursing, and banishing him from her presence.

"Your father is a fucking asshole," she would say. "I'm not saying he's a bad father, but he's a shitty husband."

I don't remember the exact moment she had him move to the basement, but it was during a time when my other friends appeared to have happily married parents in happy enough homes. In my home, though, staying together in the face of misery quickly became a twisted kind of norm.

In the 1990s, I spent my days as a high-achieving student and athlete, choreographing school plays and trying desperately to win the admiration of the swim coach, Allen, who seemed to care only about the elite swimmers (I was middle of the pack at best). At home, I worked toward getting straight As and strived for perfection to calm the unrelenting anxiety that ran rampant inside me.

I spent the evenings tuning out my parents' arguments when my father bothered to emerge upstairs. When he inevitably stormed out or retreated back to his underground lair, my mother would begin pacing the upstairs hallway in a fit of rage.

"I swear to God, if I could kill your father, I would!" she would shout, as I stood at her side. "He stole the money my father left for the two of you and now he cries poverty? Now, he wants to control our spending? Over my dead body."

She would scowl and sigh for a while and then swallow a handful of pills and slowly disappear into herself. The shift was so pronounced I could almost see her fade away. Her rage softened, her eyes glazed over, and she began stumbling around the house until she eventually passed out in her bed. Sometimes, before she fell asleep, she would stand by the kitchen counter and shovel hamantaschen cookies down her throat, unaware I was watching from the landing.

Each night, I watched from the bottom of the stairs as she shuffled up to her bedroom, a shell of the mother I knew. In those moments, I felt so afraid of who she was in the dark. Her hair was suddenly unkempt, her clothes baggy, her skin pale. She ate more food in those few obliterated minutes than she did all day, and if she spotted me watching, she looked at me like a ghost, her eyes vacant and unfamiliar.

For better or worse, my mother did not censor herself when she talked to us. When I was a young child, the stories she chose to share made me fiercely protective of her. I took her words as gospel and assumed her rants represented the full truth—she had been horribly mistreated and deserved compensation. After all the hurt she suffered, I decided I would be the one to guard her against future injury. I would monitor the people who made her cry—her mother and my father, for starters—and ask her again and again why she let them, hoping she would cut them off so she could finally be happy. And then we could be happy together. I nodded my head in vigorous agreement when she detailed my father's constant mistakes, feeling impassioned by her anger to the point that it became my own.

My sister Jessica and I were treated like adults from the get-go, a duo of listeners for her to discharge her painful past on. Our mother shared many stories of her life, including the time she first fell in love with Michael, the boyfriend who broke her heart just before she met my dad. She described a harrowing childhood, one in which her mother, Grandma Marie, criticized her constantly, calling her "fat"—all the while contending with her father's attention as he engaged in regular extramarital affairs. My mother still invited Grandma Marie over for holidays and visits, though I never understood why.

"Why do you let Grandma make you cry like that?" I would ask. The embarrassment and impatience in my mother's eyes seemed to say, *Shut up and stay quiet*, though she never answered me.

It seemed to me that my mother had learned to be a good girl, stay quiet, and follow the rules so as not to attract negative attention. When she was young, her home life was volatile (not unlike ours, but that didn't occur to me then). Her parents screamed at each other until her father left for days to get his kicks elsewhere.

During her husband's absence, my grandmother would lash out on my mother, shaming her appearance, pulling food off her plate, and yanking her hair back in a tight bun to make her look like a porcelain doll. My mother grew up in the late 1950s and early 1960s, a time when women were chastised for speaking up. Besides having no voice in her own home, my mother was a victim of the oppressive cultural expectations of the time, when marriages at a young age were expected and often predetermined, regardless of whether love existed.

My heart broke for the young version of my mother, imagining this small helpless child, abused by a mother who should have loved her and abandoned by a father who was only there when it was convenient for him, whose affection was transient. My mother missed her father terribly. He died of a brain aneurysm when I was very young. Before he died, though, he gave my mother his seal of approval to marry my dad, calling him a "good guy" and encouraging my mother to tie the knot despite the absence of romantic feelings.

"Good father, terrible husband," she would always say, shaking her head in self-pity. "Do you know I used to try holding your father's hand early on in the relationship and he would pull it away?" she'd recall angrily. "Don't make the same mistakes I did."

She felt forced into a life she didn't want with a man she didn't love. I tried to fix it, but my efforts were in vain. My mother hadn't been raised to trust her own instincts, but she got really good at becoming what others wanted her to be. (Eventually, this would become a painfully familiar pattern in my own life.) And so, early on, having never found a voice of her own, my mother said she ended up with my father because someone else told her she should. She took cues from her external environment and molded herself into a version that would keep the peace.

But by the time my sister and I came into adolescence, my mother got so sick of following the rules that all she wanted to do was break them. Never given the chance to rebel as a child, she let her untreated teen angst out with my sister and me, challenging cultural norms in reckless ways, with her middle finger held high in the air. It was as if she was the one with the impulse to act out instead of us.

My mom often took me and Jess to the local YMCA, a place where we could play and she could exercise. A nice man named Michael used to watch us, and my mom's eyes always lit up a bit at pickup time.

"How were the kids today?" she'd say, giggling and resting her palm on his shoulder. "Hopefully not too feisty!"

At some point, I remember we all went to lunch, and in between scoops of bread dipped in sunny-side-up eggs, I looked at them and said, "You two should be married." Even then, I understood my mother's discontent with my father so deeply that I was trying to pair her with someone who seemed to bring out her happy side. Decades later I would discover Michael was one of the primary men with whom she cheated on my father. Their secret relationship lasted a decade.

Whether she was cheating on my dad, abusing prescription pills (which my father still supplied to her in hopes of winning her favor), or buying new breasts with cash she found in bundles under Grandma Marie's bed after she passed away, my mother felt entitled to come and go as she pleased, refusing to shrink her desires to placate anyone. She no longer presented any kind of front to her girls. At the time, she seemed empowered. In hindsight, she was destructive.

Looking back, the irony of watching my mother try to "take back power" and live more fully is that I was watching the way she slowly died. Brainwashed by her upbringing and cultural conditioning, she remained trapped in a loveless marriage and juggled a handful of lies just to feel alive again. Over many years, I learned that love is a place where women go to die, leaving their essence in the shadows in exchange for a mediocre life that someone else told them to live. I learned that the only way to take back power was to lie and cheat. This distorted sense of control would come back to haunt me in many iterations for years to come, but in the meantime, I believed every word she said, standing beside her with fierce loyalty, ready to reckon with anyone or anything that tried to hurt her.

My teenage angst was magnified by an overexposure to drugs, sex, extramarital affairs, and uncensored narratives, which painted an ugly picture of relationships and love. "I can't leave your dad, it would be too hard on you and Jess," my mother would say, making us feel responsible for the death of her hopes, dreams, and desires.

None of this affected my sister and me positively during this pivotal time in our development, of course. My older sister, whose impulse to act out countered mine to please, would sneak home from raves as she was coming down from ecstasy on the nights my mother was high on her meds. We'd been close when we were young, sharing solidarity amid the instability, but our teenage years were miserable.

As Jess entered puberty, she began to hate what she saw in the mirror. She believed she was too fat, too ugly, and too stupid and I, the lowest on the totem pole, became her scapegoat. In her eyes, I was prettier, smarter, and stronger. And for that, there were repercussions, aggressive ones.

"What's wrong, Jessie?" I would ask when I saw her crying.

"Nothing!" she would yell, slamming a door in my face. "Leave me alone!"

I would ask again and again, unsure of what to do. Eventually, her rage outgrew her patience. She'd come after me hitting, kicking, and spitting. I would fight back as best as I could when she inevitably pushed me to the floor of my room, my only goal to get her out so I could slam my door and lock it behind me. In response, she would hoist herself against the banister to gain momentum and violently launch herself into my door. The paint would crack, chips falling to the ground. My parents were clueless.

In school, my peers saw the version of me I wanted them to see. It was like something out of a movie: I seemed pretty, popular, and confident. I could dance, I could socialize, I could get straight As. On the inside, though, I carried a heavy heart, knowing I didn't have the luxury of returning to a happy home like I sensed some of my peers did. Instead, every time I walked through our ripped screen door, I braced myself to absorb my mother's emotional outbursts, my father's persistent absence, and my sister's violence.

Even then, I somewhat unconsciously saw myself as the survivor among them. While the building might have been crumbling around me, I could stand strong, holding the weakening structures in place. From a wiring perspective, I was building feedback loops that helped me to survive. To feel safe in my home, I had to hold myself and the relationships around me together. This became a huge part of my adolescent identity—carefully focusing my attention on others at the expense of paying attention to myself.

In retrospect, my heartbreak was probably more obvious than I realized. There's only so much you can hide. Often, when I spent time with friends, I either tried to fast-track intimacy through hypersexuality or oversharing. In seventh grade, I met a girlfriend in a bathroom stall and made out with her. After, I confided in someone about it, and before the end of the day, the entire school found out.

"Lesbian!" the kids shouted at me.

I was desperate to feel close to someone and to be taken care of in any possible way. I thought love meant sharing everything, no matter how inappropriate or gory the details. In efforts to feel loved and understood, I shared intimate details of my mother's affairs and my sister's sexual escapades that should have remained private.

I operated in two worlds at once. At school I was high achieving, feared, hated, and worshipped. At home my mother struggled with constant depression and anxiety, my father swam in a sea of denial, and my sister had begun experimenting in unhealthy ways with sex and drugs. Starting at fifteen, she paved the way for normalizing underage clubbing and drug use. It wasn't long before I was using a fake ID to get into some of the most popular nightclubs in New York City, dropping ecstasy until the sun came up.

Even as it dawned on me that my household was not functioning as it should, my anger toward my father slowly ballooned. Why hadn't he asked me how I was doing or how my heart was feeling? I was the child, after all!

At home, I let my mother's word rule, never questioning her infidelity or her rage. The fact that my mother was also too busy lamenting her own circumstances to ask about my mental state didn't matter. She seemed to have suffered so much, and since she was my entire world, my goal was to make sure she was safe and happy. I would hold things together for both of us.

All through high school, my mom reminded me that getting my college degree would be my ticket out of needing anyone or anything, and that nobody could ever take it away from me. Despite my love for dance, she insisted academics were the only viable path, a surefire way to a stable life. This felt confusing because, amid all this chaos, I loved dance more than just about anything in the world, second only to my mother. It was my safe space, the only thing that brought me pure joy.

This was a pivotal moment where I was being encouraged to choose "control" over chaos, "stability" over instability. For a little while longer, my mother won this battle, and I put school ahead of dance, straight A's ahead of creativity, and my mother's fears ahead of my own passion. I felt like I had to choose between the two. If I pursued my dreams, I'd lose my mother's support and approval. But if I abandoned my dreams, I would have my mother's love. And in a child's world, nothing trumps safety.

When people started asking about what I was studying in college, I said "communications" with a smile, knowing full well it would end the conversation quickly. Even at eighteen, I found it odd that we're expected to be clear about what we want to do with our entire lives when we're the most confused about who we are. But alas, the combination of cultural expectations and my mother's teachings left me with little wiggle room to question the rules.

Ironically, much like her (or at least the narrative she shared about herself as a young person), I was a rule follower, reliant on others to guide my next steps. It was my role in the family dynamic. *Anyway*, I would tell myself, *this is just what people do—graduate high school, go to college, pick a major, and start a career.* But every time I said "communications," I betrayed myself. I had a real passion, and that wasn't it.

At the time, it was clear to me the safest choice was to get my degree, not pursue my passion. As a perfectionist, I found academics comfortable and familiar. There was a clearly prescribed path from start to finish. By now, my hardwiring had cemented a few things:

1. Men are assholes.
2. When someone hurts you, they are crossed off the list forever.
3. You can't trust anybody but yourself.

By this point, several coping mechanisms were baked into my subconscious. Because life was unpredictable at home, I learned to gaze outward before I gazed inward. I learned to prize appearances over reality. I searched for attention and recognition. I kept myself safe by seeing what was needed and becoming it. I kept myself close to my mother by being a keen observer of her discomfort, practicing how to protect her even if it meant abandoning myself in the process. I didn't know it yet, but even then, I was powerless over so much, and the tools I acquired for how to handle stress were unmanageable. For a very long time, I tried desperately to manage the mess, believing in my bones that I could fix it all.

AN ALTERNATE LOOK AT STEP ONE

As we deconstruct Step One, let's examine an example of powerlessness and unmanageability that has nothing to do with addiction. Imagine this scenario.

About five years into my sobriety, I begin to discover how to create real female friendships. They become the one thing I can rely on most often in a very shaky world. One Saturday evening,

I sit down with my best friend and listen carefully to her life update. It has been five years since her divorce, and she has had several failed relationships. Every time one ends, her negative self-talk begins anew.

"Clearly there must be something wrong with me, because everyone else seems to be able to find and keep love except for me—even stupid people," she says.

She decides to wait a while before entering the shark tank again. When asked about how she's doing, her response is an eye roll and something like, "Good in all areas except dating." She has deleted and reinstalled her dating app many times and invested heavily into the narrative that she's not worthy of a relationship.

When she sees other people in love, she feels angry and triggered—after all, she did not decide to end her marriage, though in hindsight she admits that it was probably for the best. She describes the rest of her days out in the world, a place where she shows up for her friends and her work with great consistency and rigor.

Let's consider two different paths my friend, whom we'll call Rachel, could take at this point in her dating scenario.

Reaction 1: Powerlessness (with a Death Grip on the Illusion of Control)

Rachel wakes up feeling like it's Groundhog Day. She goes to work, exercises, walks the dog, eats dinner, and binges on Netflix. She feels anxious and irritable about her empty love life. She obsesses over her past relationships and wonders what she could have said or done to make it better. *Maybe I wouldn't be single if . . .* runs rampant through her head.

She comes home from work and stalks her contemporaries and exes on Instagram, playing the dangerous game of compare and despair, gagging at other people's posts who seem madly in love with little to no effort. She deletes all her dating apps again after a near mental breakdown. She doesn't sleep well and then crashes the next night from exhaustion. When she has dinner with her friends, she talks incessantly about the terrible state of the dating scene. She cannot help but think there is something wrong with her. Even though she tries not to be upset, she is resentful of the people around her in long-term relationships. As she moves about each day, she is stuck in a feedback loop that tells her she will be alone forever.

Reaction 2: Empowerment through Admitting How Little Control Exists

Rachel wakes up five minutes earlier than usual and tries to meditate at her therapist's request. She notices her busy mind is already telling her that she will never find long-term love, and dating in Los Angeles is impossible. She tries hard to notice the thoughts and not feed them, takes a deep breath, and gets out of bed.

She considers the many things she is powerless over—for starters, these initial negative thoughts that appear in her mind. She lengthens the list. She is powerless over her divorce, her dating experience post-divorce, and her relentless desire to find love. She has proof that when she entertains negative thoughts, she spirals into a self-deprecating narrative that creates anxiety and obsession. Plainly put, when she focuses on what she is powerless over, her day becomes an unmanageable, exhausting inner dialogue of self-hatred and obsessive Google searching of things like "how to find love after divorce."

The reminder of her powerlessness and unmanageability is a way to redirect the chaos. If that leads her down a dead-end road, then the real question becomes, what does she have power over? She imagines the answers. Perhaps not her first thought, but maybe the second and third. Perhaps not the past or the future, but maybe the here and now. Perhaps not what she has lost (her marriage) but what she has gained (self-worth, dignity, and resilience). With every bad date, she gains clarity and confidence in what she wants and deserves. After this quick analysis, she feels a bit lighter and a lot more hopeful.

Wrap-Up: The Acceptance of Ambiguity

If you can relate to Reaction 1, good! It's normal to feel disheartened after so much loss. Divorce, whether wanted or not, is its own form of grief. If you're not ruminating over divorce, maybe it's a job opportunity that went to someone else, the end of a friendship you wanted to keep, or a phase of parenting you wish you could skip. Fear is part of the human condition, and it's a natural response to want to control the world around us when the fear gets too big.

When I speak in recovery rooms to people who struggle with substance abuse, I begin by saying that control is my drug of choice, and it is still true fifteen years into my sobriety. So many of us have this beautiful delusion that if we can control our worlds, we are safe. We are taught this in a variety of ways—sometimes through our upbringing, sometimes through our hardwiring, and often from societal culture. When you get the dream job, you'll be happy. When you buy your dream home, you can stop grinding. When you marry the perfect partner, you've arrived. There are constant markers for what success looks like, and we are made to believe that they are within our control.

Some goals have a clear path. If you want to be a doctor, then you take certain classes, pass exams, and enter the field. If you want to own a home, you save a little bit of money at a time and eventually have a down payment. When it comes to matters of the heart, though, nearly everything is outside our control. What is external to us feels impossible to grab because it is. We often relentlessly try to pursue things outside of ourselves because we have bought into a narrative that says, *Happiness is right over there.* When we get honest, though, the feelings of love, loss, grief, betrayal, and resentment (to name a few) require internal excavation that no outside thing, person, or situation can fix.

If you resonate with Reaction 2, all the same initial thoughts and feelings exist, but there is an attempt to widen the lens of the response. Why? Likely because the other way feels awful (and you are tired of feeling awful). On this path, we get curious about all the ways our minds want to exert power over the dating situation. Why are we convinced we will be alone forever? Why are we deleting the apps? Why are we obsessively searching on Google about love after divorce? Maybe it's because we are looking for an answer to something that doesn't have a clear trajectory. Maybe it's because matters of love require ongoing patience and flexibility. Maybe it's because the vulnerability required to "trust the process" is terrifying. Maybe we are powerless over when and where and how we will meet our next partner.

If we take this path, we can drop the armor and focus on what we *do* have some power over: our state of mind. Maybe when we have those initial thoughts we can gently say, *Hi there. I hear you, fear—thanks for sharing. Now I am going to imagine a life where I meet my partner and it's better than anything I could ever dream.* Maybe the new behavioral practice is to turn up the awareness of the controlling voice and respond as often as possible with a loving but executive voice that says, *I see you, but we're not doing this right now. Today I will leave a little space for hope about the things I cannot see.*

Why is a practice like this useful? Well, without it, the brain will keep telling the body the old story, and there will be stronger neural pathways that cement the idea that we are not worthy of love and connection. Is that what we want? If not, then the practice of heightened awareness and a new kind of self-talk creates a new feedback loop between brain and body that makes space for a new experience.

This can change the course of your entire day. You might be more hopeful, more open to connection, and more energetically aligned with your actual dream, which is to love again. Your life in the regular day to day feels more manageable because you're not beating yourself up or walking around with a chip on your shoulder. Physiologically, you are less stressed, anxious, and afraid, so your nervous system is more balanced.

The thing is, we *love* control, and it works—until it doesn't. The work, then, becomes the recognition of our own powerlessness. This is the critical first step because only when we do this can we create a blank slate for what we *do* have power over.

Let's circle back to the first path related to our scenario. Feeling hopeless and angry about being single is normal and understandable, but when we feed that narrative and try to control outcomes to force a new narrative, it doesn't work. We tell ourselves a story that we will be alone forever because even *that* is a form of control, right? If that story is true, the path is clear once again. We can give up dating altogether and focus on other things because we are destined to be single anyway. This is the way our fear and ego keep us sick, stuck, and not living joyfully, prisoner to the voice inside that says it won't work out.

When we do this, we give our power away to our fear instead of getting curious about what it's trying to teach us. The irony of real change is that you must be so sick and tired of the way you've been living that you are willing to try something new. You must be more afraid to go on the way you have than to change.

STEP ONE: MY VERSION

The following is an activity inspired by Step One of the Twelve Steps. As a reminder, in Step One, I have admitted I am powerless over alcohol and drugs and that my life has become unmanageable.[3] This is the first step in the rewiring process, and I use the relationship with my mother to illustrate how we can implement it into our daily lives.

Where in my childhood am I powerless?

- Over my mother's limited beliefs
- Over my mother's eating disorder
- Over my mother's pill addiction
- Over my mother's traumatic childhood
- Over my mother oversharing her personal life

Where in this part of my story did my life become unmanageable? Why?

- When I tried to fix and save my mother
- When I put my own needs aside for the sake of others
- When I used the idea that "the only person I can count on is myself" as a mantra for living

Where in hindsight do I actually have some power?

- Over my own actions and behaviors
- Over separating what parts of the story are mine and what are my mother's
- Over practicing forgiveness and compassion for my mom's limitations
- Over reconciling what wasn't fair about my upbringing as a child and taking responsibility for what I can as an adult

---

3   Alcoholics Anonymous World Services, *Twelve Steps and Twelve Traditions*, 21.

STEP ONE: YOUR VERSION

Fill in the blank: I have admitted I am powerless over _____

_____, and my life has become unmanageable in the

following ways: _____.

1. With Step One in mind, write down five things you are powerless over. This can be anything: people, places, situations, institutions. Get as granular and creative as you'd like.

2. Then write down five things that are unmanageable in your life, particularly when you try and exert power over them. (If you're unsure, consider these examples: nagging your partner about the same thing over and over; googling something for the hundredth time and expecting to find a new answer.)

3. Write down five things you *do* have power over. If, for example, you have power over your responses, then what would that look like? If normally you react in a way that you aren't proud of, but you realize you have power over how you respond, what would be required to do it differently? Would you need to take a long, deep breath first? Call a friend? Sleep on it before saying anything?

Use your imagination to dream up a new and better world in these scenarios. And next time you find yourself in one of them, *practice* what you wrote! This is a slow and steady method of change, but I promise that tiny habits practiced consistently lead to massive shifts. One behavior change at a time, we can create new experiences and, on the other side, access a new kind of freedom.

2

BE YOU

WELCOME TO STEP TWO IN the recovery of self:

[We] came to believe that a Power greater than
ourselves could restore us to sanity.[4]

Before you close the book, hear me out. I realize that upon first reading, this step might sound religious, dated, or downright offensive. You might be thinking, *Who or what is this Power? And why are you calling me insane?* When I first read this step in early sobriety, it repulsed me. As an atheist, not only did I despise the idea of a "higher power," but to then be asked to have that power fix my insanity was downright infuriating. I truly saw no way through this step, and yet I also knew I couldn't drink or use drugs anymore.

I have a knack for keeping something in a stranglehold until it looks exactly how I want it to look. The only trouble with this philosophy is that life is in session, and most of it is out of my control. If I spend my precious time trying to make it go exactly according

4   Alcoholics Anonymous World Services, *Twelve Steps and Twelve Traditions* (New York: Alcoholics Anonymous World Services, 1981), 25.

to plan, not only am I expending a lot of energy, but I am also losing access to real power—the kind that comes when you have inner peace regardless of your outside circumstances.

But I get it—this step can be off-putting. I remember hearing it in AA and thinking two distinct things:

1. I'm not insane, thank you very much.
2. What magical power in the sky is going to wave
   a wand and strike me sane if I'm acting crazy?

Not only did the language turn me off, but the message also felt impossible because I came from a home where I learned that the only person I could count on was myself.

As a young girl, my willpower was everything. It helped me keep my chin up in the face of bullying, my grades high in the face of failing, and my mother happy in the face of heartbreak. When it came to drugs and alcohol, I used my willpower repeatedly and in the beginning it worked wonders. Work hard, play hard. I studied, held down a job, and stayed fit, all while partying on the weekends. Then, like magic, I cleaned up my act for the start of a new week. My hardwiring for perfection made self-reliance natural—I was perfectly capable of controlling the world around me. Plus, my mother reinforced this belief by shunning the idea of God as something the weak and vulnerable rely on when they have no backbone.

THE PROBLEM WITH RELYING ON NO ONE ELSE

When I went off to college at Boston University, it felt like my whole world opened. I felt free from the dysfunction of my childhood and began questioning everything my mother taught me. Was cheating okay if your partner treated you badly? Was my dad actually an asshole? Would prescription medication solve my problems if they got too big?

As nice as it was to explore new ideas, I still relied heavily on my wiring for perfection to make me feel safe and whole. I studied constantly and only let myself drink and smoke weed occasionally on the weekends to unwind. I ate healthier than ever so I could come back thinner, showing everyone that the Freshman Fifteen didn't apply to me. All was well until I saw Jake—a six-foot-four man with a thick, curly brown Afro—glide down the dormitory corridors in a bathrobe like he owned the damn place. *Who the fuck is that?* I wondered. From that moment, I made sure to time my lunchroom arrivals with his until eventually I said hello. I came undone every time we spoke. My insides swirled with a nervous excitement as we sat down to eat, my mind buzzing with the type of fireworks reserved only for a new kind of love. I had never felt anything like this before—a true dopamine explosion that felt impossible to live without.

"I don't believe in monogamy," Jake said, biting into a BLT dripping with mayo. "I believe there is value in growing with just one person, but I'm so young that I think there's more value in growing a little bit with a lot of people." He licked his lips.

I will change your mind, I thought. *And I will kiss those lips soon.*

There wasn't a shred of doubt that I would be the one to reroute his belief about monogamy. He hadn't met a girl like me before, and once he realized how special I was, I was sure he would commit. In the meantime, we spent more and more time together. We laughed, we fucked, we smoked weed, and we dreamed of a better world.

By sophomore year, it was as though we were exclusive, just without the label. Occasionally he would disappear, and I would stare relentlessly at my phone waiting for him to text. At this point, we were spending almost every night together, fucking without a condom, and talking openly about how we could still see other people. I played it cool because I couldn't imagine a world without him, and I kept trying to trust that he didn't give us a label because he was afraid, not because he didn't care.

I tried putting my focus back on my studies and that mostly worked, except for one writing class where the professor refused to give me anything other than a C. My wiring pushed me deeper into wanting to control my grades and my relationship—ruminating and obsessing over how to get this professor and Jake to love me more. As I struggled to perform at the level I was accustomed to, I decided to do online research for my next writing assignment. I came across a fabulous movie review about *American Beauty*, one of my all-time favorites.

Without intending to cheat, I took large chunks of the review and never cited my sources. I handed in my paper and spent the next several nights sleeping at Jake's place, all while dating other people—so I could prove to myself that I wasn't a total fool. When I went back to my writing class, the professor handed back my paper, and it had a big red zero on top, followed by a "See me after class." I immediately panicked, and as the classroom emptied, his eyes met mine with disdain.

"Do you see what I have stapled here behind your work?" he asked.

I shook my head, feeling my stomach in my throat.

"It's the paper you plagiarized. You see, this piece of writing was so much better than your other work, I wondered how that was possible. So I searched some of the sentences from your paper, and up popped this movie review. I will be taking this to the administrative board and will notify you of what's next," he said.

In one instant, my world changed forever. I dreaded the inevitable call to my mother, the weight of her disappointment seeping into my nervous system. Her brilliant daughter with a 3.8 GPA was caught plagiarizing at a major university. This would be the collapse of all her dreams for me and what I thought were all of mine. I agonized over her potential reaction, finally succumbing with a phone call later that afternoon.

"Mom, I have to tell you something and it's not good."

Silence.

"What, Sammy? Just tell me," she pleaded.

"I made a huge mistake. I didn't mean to do it, but I plagiarized because I never cited my sources, and I have to go in front of a committee. I don't know what's going to happen," I sobbed.

"Oh God," she said. "Sam, how could you do this? What are we going to do?"

In the background, I heard her whisper to Ben, her alcoholic boyfriend, who mumbled something back that I couldn't make out.

"Ben said we can fix this," my mom said. "He wants to talk to you."

He cleared his gurgled throat.

"Sam, your mom and I know you're a great kid and a great student, and this is clearly a mistake. We will make a great case, and we will prove them wrong. Don't worry," he said confidently.

I wondered if he was drunk or not and told them I would call them later. I hung up and cried, squeezing my pillow and watching mascara spread across the white pillowcase. I clutched it desperately, snot dripping from my nose, as though my effort would prevent me from falling through the earth.

Looking back, this would have been a wonderful time to have a relationship with a power greater than myself to help restore me to sanity. There were so many opportunities before this moment when I could have pivoted. As my anxiety revved up in the class, I could have asked the teacher for more support. I could have gotten a tutor. I could have done my best, even if it was only getting me a C, and practiced acceptance around not having to be the best all the time. But I didn't have those skills. My circuitry was wired for success at all costs, perfection rather than progress, and control over people, places, and things in the face of uncertainty.

Instead of getting honest and vulnerable about how deeply I was struggling, I obsessed over what to do, what to say, and how to fix it. This had to go away. It was a mistake, after all. I never went into the assignment intending to plagiarize. I just wanted to get an A. I just wanted to be good enough.

The academic committee at BU decided I could plead my case in a hearing. Ben had worked tirelessly on a script he wanted me to follow, promising that if I said these words exactly, I could prove my innocence. As the day of the hearing crept closer, my anxiety went through the roof. I knew I had messed up, and I just wanted to tell the truth. But Ben insisted I stick to the script and swore to my mother and I that if I practiced my argument, my punishment would be minimal, and this would all go away.

For weeks, I studied the lines he prepared for me. It wasn't plagiarism in the traditional sense, he reminded me, it was unintentional. I simply forgot to cite my sources. I had no desire to cheat or pretend my work was better than what it was. This type of gaslighting was not the first time I abandoned my intuition in favor of something (or someone) outside of myself. As my insides screamed, *Just be honest!*, outside forces shouted, *No, we can fix this and make it go away! Nothing happened!* Clueless and terrified, I followed instructions like a good little soldier.

Because my circuitry was wired to ignore my own needs, I had no reason to trust my insides. Standing before the committee, I said words that meant nothing to me and watched myself argue in defense of my actions. I spouted off all my accolades at the university, including winning the distinguished sophomore award for high grades—promising that the award was earned and not forged.

"I am a tried-and-true student who loves working hard," I began. I watched their faces fall flat as I spoke; I left the room praying to a God I didn't believe in.

They decided to suspend me for eighteen months. They did not expel me, which would have been on my permanent record, but I could only come back when all my friends would be in their final semester of their senior year. It was a crushing blow—first to my mother's ego and her boyfriend's self-righteous denial, and second to my authentic self. Somewhere in there I knew I was good and that this was a bad decision made by a good person. But it would be a long time before the shame and guilt of that decision would lift.

Here I was, an eighteen-year-old girl who had learned to perform and perfect at all costs, now being asked to leave campus for a year and a half because the idea of failing was intolerable to me. I had tried so hard to follow the "If this, then that" rules. If I study, then I will get good grades. If I get good grades, then I will get a good job. If I get a good job, then I will have a stable life.

No one prepared me for the gray version of "If this, then maybe." If I study, I may or may not get an A, but as long as I try my best, it is good enough. If I get good grades, I might apply to a desired job and get the position, or I might have to keep trying until I find something that works, which is fine as long as it makes me feel good inside. And if I get a good job, then I might be able to afford some more material things, but there is no guarantee that I will be happy. I could hate it, I could quit it, and I could decide to go in an entirely new direction. And even if the path looks wildly different than I had originally planned, I could *still be okay*. If I had practiced the art of trusting something or someone besides myself, asking for help and tolerating failure, then the entire course of my life could have changed.

Romantically, things weren't much different. Despite my best efforts to control things, Jake still saw other people even as we spent countless nights together at his off-campus apartment. He was very supportive about my academic mishaps; he had gone through something similar with a girl named Jane a couple of years earlier. I didn't know much about her, but I knew he was fond of her, and I knew they had traveled together during their suspension. Supposedly they were just friends now, but for some reason, she was the one person I feared the most in our open relationship—the one person I thought he loved besides me. Our time together became so frequent, we agreed to become sexually exclusive. Finally, I thought, I can have him all to myself.

As my sophomore year was coming to its traumatic close and Jake's graduation was just days away, I shacked up with him as often as I could. After a night of dancing with friends, I planned to go to his place. I called incessantly, expecting him to answer. He never picked up. It was so odd after spending every waking second together, I struggled to fall asleep that night. After not hearing from him the next morning, my mind spun with thoughts of where he was and with whom. No matter how conditioned I had become to accept the terms of the open relationship, my hardwiring showed up as I obsessively tried to figure out his whereabouts.

I googled "things to do off campus before graduation" and "how to tell if your boyfriend is cheating on you" before closing my laptop and leaving the dorm room in a silent fury. Over the next few hours of my life, I spun into a rage, possessed by an insatiable appetite for control. I nearly ran over to his apartment and, like an insane person, peered through his window at every angle to see if his room looked used up or untouched. The lights were off, and his oversized mattress was resting vertically against the frame. It was official. No matter what he would tell me, I knew he hadn't come home last night. When he slept at home, the mattress was set up on the floor in the morning—his live/sleep solution, since he was too damn cheap to upgrade his bed frame so it would fit the mattress.

There was only one conclusion I could draw: Jane. In an instant, the life I had built over the past two years shattered. When Jake finally called me at 2:00 p.m., cool and casual, I flew off the handle.

"Where the fuck were you last night?" I shouted.

He tried to play it off. I finally stopped acting okay when I wasn't.

"Stop lying, Jake! I know you were with her. Just fucking tell me."

I was right. And when I asked if they had slept together, they had. And when I asked if they used protection, they hadn't. I hung up the phone and felt everything collapse under me. Every single ounce of effort and energy to be perfect, loved, and understood in the past two years was gone. Irrelevant. Incapable of saving me from this agony.

A few months after moving back home, I tested positive for HPV. Jane had it and gave it to Jake, who gave it to me. A final, crushing blow to a tumultuous year.

This was one of the many rock bottoms in my life where my persistent desire to keep things neat and orderly had failed miserably, where my wiring for perfection ended up harming rather than helping me. When you're raised to use perfection and control as a survival mechanism to have your needs met, it takes some thawing out to rewire your nervous system and teach your body that you are safe without those tools. That in fact, you are in more danger using them to navigate life's adversities than you are in putting them down.

When I think of Step Two now, it lands differently. At some point after trying rigorously to hold on to my own beliefs, I started to ask myself new questions: Can I come to believe that something besides my own circuitry and desire for control can help alleviate my suffering? Can I recognize and break the cycle of insanity when I continue to do the same things again and again and expect different results? Can I create a new core belief that perhaps something outside of my ego, fear, and perfectionism might guide me to a more joyful outcome? The answer is yes—but not without reaching sheer desperation first.

For many years, I fumbled my way through Step Two, borrowing someone else's faith in a power I could not see or feel or touch. I also didn't truly buy into the idea that I was crazy—misguided, perhaps, but not insane. Even after the dramatic end of my time at Boston University, I went on to have a job, a boyfriend, and more straight A's at the subsequent university I ended up in. It was a long time before I understood the true depth and weight of this step, and even longer before I unhooked myself from the religious implications embedded in it. I was several years into recovery before I understood the ultimate purpose of Step Two—the surrendering of our will when we are beating something to the ground in exchange for inner peace. A more joyful life. Comfort in the discomfort. Forget about God for a moment; this step is about learning how to feel good in our own skin.

AN ALTERNATE LOOK AT STEP TWO

Imagine this scenario. I am in the middle of studying for a huge exam, one for which the outcome means the start of a new career or staying in one that I hate. I walk into my house, find dishes piled up in the sink, and see dirty clothes spread across the floor. Then, my mother, who has untreated bipolar disorder, sends me eight texts in a row about how she is going to be a millionaire in the next three months because she met a man who promised that he could make her rich. My partner asks how my day was.

"I'd love to tell you about it after I clean up this mess," I say sharply.

His face hardens. "What's your problem?"

I glare, unleashing my fury. "Oh, I don't know, maybe my problem is that I need a partner who actually cleans the fucking house without me asking because he knows it's important to me! Maybe my problem is that I married someone who I have to fucking babysit instead of a real partner who gets shit done!"

A huge fight ensues. I storm off, feeling awful about the massive communication breakdown.

What is actually happening here? Well, I am emotionally overwhelmed, for starters. When I take a step back and examine the situation, I realize a few things:

1. I have been studying for an exam that I really want to pass, but whether I do is totally out of my control besides the effort I put into the studying itself.

2. I love the feeling of a clean and tidy house because I like it when my outsides match my insides. In other words, I want the house to be neat because it makes me feel less out of control on the inside.

3. My mother has suffered from mental illness my entire life, and at the moment, she is in an acute manic episode and refusing to take her meds. Her texts are a painful reminder that I do not have emotional or physical autonomy over anyone besides myself and that her sickness hurts my heart.

4. I feel absolutely powerless.

There are many ways the fallout of this interaction could have gone down. Let's play out the version in which I had no tools and the version in which I did (and I actually used them).

Reaction 1: A Reaction Rather Than a Response

I march into the bedroom full of rage. After letting out a huge scream, I ramble curse words under my breath and mentally rant about my inadequate partner. *Every time I ask for something—a clean house, a warm meal—it feels like he lets me down. The floors are still dirty, the food tastes like shit.* I remember my mother's words: *The only person you can count on is yourself.* I resolve, once again, to take on the burden myself. *I will cook, I will clean, I will land the job.*

Even though I am exhausted from carrying the financial and mental load, I feel like I have no choice. I believe in every bone of my body that if I don't do it, it won't get done. I stockpile my resentment on top of the others I've accumulated. After all, this is the partner and the life I chose. *Suck it up and deal with it*, I tell myself. I head back out into the living room and start cleaning up, and when my partner tries to connect with me, I am emotionally shut down.

"I'm fine," I say.

After I clean up, we sit on the couch and watch Netflix as if nothing ever happened.

Reaction 2: The Power of Self-Regulation

I walk away angry and overwhelmed. I turn on the shower, and as the water warms up, I pace around my bedroom and try to keep my head from exploding. I am not crazy; I have asked for help at home many times and it never seems to get better. But I also realize my partner loves me, and even though he isn't good at cleaning up he is really good at a lot of other things. I undress and stand under the water, trying to play back what the hell just happened.

I had a hard day where everything felt wildly out of my control—my career, my house, my mother's mental state. When I got home, I desperately wanted everything to look and feel a certain way so that at least something was within my control. When home didn't look the way I wanted it to, I lost it. As a result of pushing my will on to someone else and not getting what I wanted, I felt afraid. I discharged that fear on to my partner. I blamed him for the way things are, when, in fact, no amount of cleanliness changes the things I fear. Even if the house were spotless, I wouldn't know about the job, and my mother would still be unstable.

In my self-reflection, I realize that I bypassed my own feelings and pointed the finger outward because blaming someone else gave me the illusion that I was back in control. Realizing this makes me feel a sense of anxiety and shame. When I think of how to apply Step Two to this scenario, I break it down based on the life situation I am in. What power do I believe is directing me right now? Clearly, I believe that I am the authority figure making all these things happen. I have to pass the exam so I will land the job; I have to keep the house clean, or it stays a mess; and I have to monitor my mother's behavior, or she might hurt herself or someone else. Or do I? And then, do I feel calm and clear when I am trying to control these elements in my life? It sure doesn't seem like it, based on how I reacted.

I ask myself, *What if I reframe it?* What if, in this scenario, a "power greater than me" was the power to ask for help from my partner? What if the power was simply something larger than my ego. How would that play out?

I might walk in overwhelmed by the pending exam and see the mess. In response, I might say to my partner, "I am feeling so overwhelmed by this exam. I could really use your help cleaning up so I have one less thing to do as I prepare."

Because I come from a loving place, his response will likely be loving in return. "Sure," he says. "And just in case you need to hear it, you're doing a great job. The questions aren't up to you but the way you prepare is, and you've prepared a lot. I'm proud of you."

Let's look at my mother's text messages. I could respond, but that would be insanity—doing the same thing again and again and expecting different results. I know she is not well. If I try to "get her to see" that she is delusional and the man she met is bullshitting her, she will write me back in a manic state, spouting off grand delusions and interpreting my lack of confidence in her ability as my desire for her to be unhappy. Instead, I might put my phone away and take a long, deep breath, stating the Serenity Prayer: *God, grant me the serenity to accept the things [people, places, situations, reactions, opinions] I cannot change, the courage to change the things [my attitude, behavior, and actions] I can, and the wisdom to know the difference.* (Note: The word "God" can be omitted or replaced with the word of your choice.)

If I'm really working Step Two, I think about the things I cannot change: whether my preparation for the exam will be enough to pass the test; that my partner doesn't value a clean house the way I do; and that my mother is in an acute manic episode. Then I think about what I can change: I can work through my anxiety about the exam by calming my nervous system through deep breathing, gentle movement, or practicing an act of self-care before responding to my mother's mental illness. I can ask myself what I *need* right now. Do I need space before writing her back or do I need complete detachment until she is well? Is there a boundary I can set while she is in this state? Can I let myself feel the grief of the healthy mother that is currently gone?

Wrap-Up: What's the Lesson Here?

This type of self-reflection requires two hard things: rigorous self-awareness and vulnerability. But as we make a start, the larger message within the step is simply the notion that we don't have to do this thing called life alone. That we were never meant to. That maybe, instead of relying on things outside of us to feel in control, we can lean into our community and our higher consciousness to work through our discomfort. One step at a time, we can retrain our nervous system to tolerate distress. We can ask for help. We can take a deep breath, cry, and rest. We can be more honest when we are struggling. Slowly, we can start to have a new experience. Slowly, we can remind our bodies that there is another way. Slowly, we create new neural pathways in the presence of feeling wildly out of control so that our bodies have a reference point the next time we inevitably want to control and manage our worlds to feel safe.

Whether you're an addict or not, we all have the same universal experiences of love, loss, and uncertainty. The thing is, when you stay sober for a while, the Steps become about the business of living. Your happiness is contingent on your emotional sobriety. I rarely get triggered to drink or use drugs these days. That said, I frequently get triggered emotionally by a husband who gets home late, a messy house, or a mentally unstable mother. The Twelve Steps have universal truths baked into them, regardless of your suffering.

In my case, if I rely on sheer willpower, then I will run things into the ground until they break. Then, in that despair, the likelihood of a relapse increases, and all bets are off. One glass of wine could turn into an eight ball of cocaine by 4:00 a.m. But what about the nonaddicts? I know plenty of people who bulldoze their way through life, using control over people, places, and things to feel a sense of safety and worthiness. This inability to surrender to something bigger than the ego can also end in disaster.

Maybe your version of suffering is existing in a relationship that you know isn't right, but you're too afraid to end. Maybe your version of running things into the ground is saying yes to everyone when you want to say no. Without a spiritual framework, how would you cope with those feelings? Maybe you drink a nightcap to take the edge off. Maybe you scroll Instagram for two hours before bed. Maybe you spend money you don't really have or perfect the thing you want to say to someone so they will finally do what you want. These micro-habits run rampant in our lives, and they are the subconscious mechanisms that create cycles of dysfunction in the nervous system.

The physical and emotional body have an eerily similar presentation. After owning a private practice for a decade, I treated dozens of patients who would come in bewildered at how they got hurt. "I don't get it. Everything was fine, and then I threw my back out when I bent over to tie my shoes," they'd say.

But that's just it. Everything is usually not fine. Depending on how we move our bodies, feed our bodies, rest our bodies, and so on, we are accumulating wear and tear a little at a time. We are chipping away, often unintentionally, at our healthy body by living our lives—either not knowing what we could be doing better or ignoring the signals our body is giving to us. The emotional body is the same. When we spend our days trying to control the world around us, disconnecting from ourselves and others, and numbing out so we don't have to do the hard work of speaking up, feeling our feelings, and asking for what we need, we slowly chip away at our emotional well-being and our sense of self-worth. We slowly teach the nervous system that to survive we must be in control or numb out.

So, is that as big of a deal as an addict taking a drink or a drug? Not immediately, no. But these behaviors accumulate over time, putting your nervous system in distress and placing distance between you and the people you love, leaving you feeling more alone and disconnected. They reinforce the "If this, then that" circuitry. If my world feels unstable, then I will control it. But when we loosen our grip, we teach the body that even when the world feels wildly unsafe, there are other options.

Sure, there is the "do it all myself" option, an old, familiar place we relied on for survival. When that runs its course, though, we become willing to try another way. We can practice asking for help, calming our nervous system, and feeling our feelings. Yes, the latter requires more courage, but it ultimately leaves us feeling more supported and connected to the people we love. This is the essence of Step Two, and this type of framework is available to all of us, every day.

Pretty great, right?

STEP TWO: YOUR VERSION

Now we will spend some time taking Step Two and making it relevant to your specific life.

As a reminder, Step Two is coming to believe that a power greater than ourselves can restore us to sanity.[5]

Get out your pen and paper, and fold it into two columns. At the top of the left side, write, "What I Am Trying to Control." At the top of the right side, write, "How This Makes Me Feel." Ask yourself the following questions, and fill out the left column:

- Where in your current life have you been holding on to something so tightly—an outcome, a person, or a behavior— that it is making you feel crazy?
- Where in your life are you trying to control and manage a person, place, thing, or situation so that it goes according to your plan, so much so that you're wreaking havoc all around you and inside of you?

Write down every single thing you're trying to control. Get specific—write down all the ways in which you are trying to control each thing. Then, across from each item, write down how it makes you feel. Is it anxious? Afraid? Exhausted?

Now, take a new piece of paper and fold it into two columns again. At the top of the left side, write, "How I Want to Feel." Label the top of the right side, "Ways to Help Me Get There." Now ask yourself this question and complete the left column: How do I want to feel as I move through my day? For example, I want to feel calm, confident, and connected.

Move to the right column now and answer the following: What are some things I can say, do, or practice to help get me closer to

---

5 Alcoholics Anonymous World Services, *Twelve Steps and Twelve Traditions*, 25.

the feelings I *want* to experience? Here are some ideas: You can pray, meditate, go for a walk, move your body, call someone you love, close your eyes and rest, journal, or get off social media for twenty-four hours.

Take a deep breath and try to practice one of these new behaviors. It may feel foreign, even terrifying. Our bodies love the coping skills they know, even when they're toxic. They are well rehearsed and familiar. In practicing something new, we kick up confusion, fear, and anxiety. We are confronted with a very important decision: Am I willing to trade my happiness for my comfort or am I sick and tired of being sick and tired? If you're ready, then you just have to jump. Take a tiny step in a new direction. Prove to yourself that you can survive and start building up a new sense of self-worth. I promise, healthy practice makes permanent. And truth be told, we only get good at what we practice.

3

THE GIFT OF DESPERATION

I'M GOING TO BE HONEST; Step Three threw me for a loop for years. I can laugh about it now, but when I was less recovered, the language of this step kept me from achieving any real emotional sobriety for a very long time.

> [We] made a decision to turn our will and our lives over to the care of God as we understood Him [or Her or It].[6]

Depending on what you were taught about God, this step can feel comforting, triggering, or anything in between. And if you were taught that your willpower is the one thing that you can count on for survival, then you have no reason to believe that giving this willpower to some random entity you can't see or feel or know will save you.

When I first read this step, I thought it sounded as insane as

---

6   Alcoholics Anonymous World Services, *Twelve Steps and Twelve Traditions* (New York: Alcoholics Anonymous World Services, 1981), 34.

Step Two. It seemed to be directing me to say, "Dear random God in the sky (that isn't real), let me give you my life on some altar, and you can take it from here." Here I am, a raging atheist, sitting in the back of meetings being told that God will save me. That without God, I have no chance of recovery. In my mind, though, I didn't drink like an alcoholic. I didn't look like an alcoholic. In fact, I didn't see, hear, or feel anything that resembled me in those rooms. And now the program wanted me to become a devout believer in God? Hell no.

But let's reframe the step so it's not dripping with religious implications. Let's excavate the words so we can extract the spiritual principles underneath. Suppose we think of Step Three this way: You have tried this thing, whatever it is, again and again, and it keeps not working. No matter how many of your internal resources you draw on, you keep feeling stuck, powerless, and angry. You feel disconnected from yourself and your loved ones and exhausted from the weight of your resentments. You know you are a smart person, but you've reached the end of your intellectual limits regarding how to solve this problem. You are tired enough to surrender and curious enough to interrogate.

As you put your hands up, you consider reaching out to people in your support system. With a deep breath and a lot of courage you might say, "I can't keep living this way. I need help and I don't know where to start." Suppose your friends hear you and hold space for you. You will likely feel better, armed with a renewed sense of hope amid the fear.

After more than a decade in recovery, this is how I interpret Step Three so it feels more modern and less rigid: *I am now willing to consider the possibility that I don't have all the answers, and from that flexible place I want to receive guidance about whatever the next right thing is.* If you try that language, how does it feel in your body?

Let's take financial fear as a fairly universal struggle. Let's imagine that you want to earn more money. Exhausted from trying several things that failed, you might be brave enough (or desperate enough) to ask for help. You might realize that you can't do this alone. You might open up to the possibility that there is another way to make things work than what you've tried. Perhaps the next action is journaling about it and then getting a good night's sleep. Perhaps you call some trusted friends and ask for their feedback. Perhaps you sign up for a course on building your financial portfolio with someone successful whom you respect and admire.

Whatever you do, you are now officially in the act of practicing new behavior. This is the exact process by which we create new feedback loops between brain and body so that we can have a new experience in our lives. These micro-shifts have macro results—we just have to be consistent.

Despite our best efforts, willpower alone cannot cure a broken heart or a distressed mind, as much as we wish it could. Depending on our hardwiring and upbringing, the process of "letting go" of a person, place, thing, or situation when it is not going your way can be anywhere from relatively easy to downright impossible. We have ingrained neurological patterns, most of which are formed very early on in our development. The brain-body connection strengthens as we rely on these feedback loops, and then we enter adulthood and continue to pound the pavement using these old patterns.

Inevitably, though, life throws a curveball, and we are confronted with something we have never navigated before—a cheating partner, a sick friend, or the loss of a loved one. It makes total sense that we would rely on the neurological pathways we have used before to navigate this new territory. The trouble is, the more emotionally complex and spiritually disarming the situation is, the less our old ways of coping help. To put it plainly, perfectionism collapses with matters of the heart.

LESSONS IN LETTING GO OF A STRANGLEHOLD

I have many things that I tried to manage by myself, which I now realize kept me very sick. A prime example of self-reliance-gone-wrong was during my active addiction. My dependency on drugs was moving faster than my ability to control it.

A year after my suspension from BU, I met Ryan. "I'm going to be famous," I told him, tossing my hair and smiling up at him. "You're either down for the ride or you're out."

Ryan found this boldness in me, this fearlessness, intoxicating at first, exciting. I dragged him to swingers' clubs and after parties and pressed his face against piles of cocaine. There was nothing I wouldn't try, and I expected him to keep up. For almost two years, he did, and then one day, after a taxi ride back to our shitty, rat-infested New York apartment, he looked at me flatly and said, "I don't want to do this anymore." He was done with the parties, the drugs, and the group sex. He was done with this wild lifestyle, the late nights, the broken promises. He was interested in building a life with me, and I was interested in building a life with cocaine. In that moment, as dawn rose over the skyline, the foundation of our relationship cracked.

Though I loved him madly, I wasn't ready to settle down or stop experimenting with drugs. I still had lots of acting out to do. So I kept up pretenses instead. I made a conscious decision to keep going, partying when and with whom I wanted, hiding my drug use and sexual affairs from him. I refused to tame the animal inside of me that wanted the lights, the fame, the glitter and the gold.

Between my mother's teachings about self-righteous anger and my intrinsic perfectionism, I fully believed I could do whatever I wanted and stay in control. I roamed free, hiding the wild animal from him, kissing and fucking other people and then sneaking back home with a pounding heart after a night of cocaine. In the dark, I swallowed copious amounts of Tylenol PM and slid under the sheets, holding Ryan's wrist long enough until my pulse matched his. As my addiction progressed, these were some of the loneliest times of my life.

The secrets and lies continued for months, and I became less mindful about hiding the truth. I got sloppy. In a grand effort to exist in two places at once, a phenomenon that I'd seen modeled and embodied all throughout my childhood, I would toast with wine over an expensive dinner with Ryan before sending a text message to one of my side pieces. I was becoming more reckless by the day, and sometimes I accidentally sent those messages to Ryan. Attempting to override feelings of powerlessness, my inner controller doubled down and tried to hide my drinking and drugging more effectively.

Because of my wiring, I swung from feelings of grandiosity to utter self-disdain. I felt trapped by Ryan's desire to love me well, but then rejected by his distaste for my wild side. That was part of me too, after all. And it was a side he had begun to hate—which I only noticed in the moments when I was sober enough to care.

Years of lying and cheating had created a sinkhole of resentment that was bubbling inside him. Still, I truly thought he would always be around because he always had been before. I took him for granted, while seeking out the drug dealers who inevitably hung by the end of the bars where I worked. Their jaws would wiggle, and I would hold their gaze until it met mine, letting them know in a single tip of my head that I was down to party. I loved Ryan and I wanted to be good for him, but I loved cocaine more.

One December day, I lost control.

I had just been accepted into a prestigious graduate program for physical therapy, and to celebrate I made plans with a woman named Heather, whom I had met one other time.

She was both a stranger and a comrade. I didn't know anything personal about her, but I knew that she partied like I did, and that made her a partner in crime. She was someone who cosigned my addiction and did cocaine like I did, so any shame that popped up around my behavior was easily buried.

Ryan had left town to visit his family for Christmas, and the plan was for me to visit my family on Christmas Eve and then meet up with him on Christmas Day. It was perfect. Get loaded, get it together, get on the road. Lather, rinse, repeat. A control freak's dream. I had no idea that on that day with Heather, my belief that I could hold it all together would shatter.

Heather came to my walk-up apartment in Hell's Kitchen and said, "Hi, gorgeous. There's a rat in the trash cans out front. Want me to call the dealer?"

As we waited for our drugs, we laughed at the ridiculous way New Yorkers lived just to be near what it offered, gossiping to kill the time before getting our fix. When a discreet-looking black car pulled up out front, Heather got in and shut the door. The risk of hopping into a stranger's car to buy drugs was not lost on me; it's just that the reward seemed worth it. When she came back inside, she had bought enough cocaine to last us all day. We started snorting lines as thick as crayons at 2:00 p.m., as if the world was our playground. It was wintertime, and the city was buzzing with energy, so we set out on a holiday shopping trip. Hustlers on the sidewalks were selling bags and hats and shirts. Outdoor shops were flickering with lights and decorative trinkets for the holidays. In between stops on our spending spree, we snorted rails of cocaine off dirty bathroom stalls. To keep the buzz going, we slurped down an occasional Corona and kept on trucking.

When we ran out of hands to hold our gifts, we came back to the apartment to wrap them (and snort more lines). Heather was tweaking with excitement to gift wrap, but my head started to feel foggy, as if clouds were hastily rolling in before an approaching storm. I went into my bedroom to watch TV and rest. I stood up on the bed to grab the remote, which hung beside the tiny television we kept in the closet. The next thing I remember is opening my eyes and seeing the world sideways, sprawled out on the floor with Heather hovering above me.

As my gaze shifted to vertical, Heather's eyes looked as if she had seen a ghost. Her pupils were dilated, and her cell phone was glued to one ear. "I don't know her address!" she pleaded. All at once, I realized she was on the phone with 911 and that something awful must have happened. A tidal wave of shame enveloped me—did I almost die? I begged her to get off the phone, convincing her that I was perfectly fine. She complied, though reluctant, and told me she had heard a loud thump and found me on the floor of my bedroom convulsing. I'd swatted her face with my arms as she tried to pull my tongue out of my throat so I didn't choke.

I was horrified. I felt ashamed that I had lost control and terrified that my drinking and drugging might have to come to an end. What did this mean? If this was an overdose, then aren't I deep into a drug addiction that is out to kill me? What about how well I held it all together? I had just gotten accepted into a doctoral program, for God's sake.

Heather and I had a mutual friend named Beth, who lived ten blocks south. I told Heather to call Beth and have her come over to smooth things out. She could verify that I was okay and mitigate any ideas about sending me to the hospital, which would have been the ultimate failure for a perfectionist struggling with addiction. Beth would assure us I was fine and therefore my addiction was not serious. She rushed to the apartment and sat beside me.

"Hey, Sammy, you all right?" she asked lovingly.

I nodded my head vigorously to assure her I was fine and whatever happened was a close call, but not an emergency. All I needed was a good night's sleep. Heather left, Beth tucked me in, and when the door to my apartment shut, I sat in front of the mirror and zeroed in on the gash across my chin—evidence of my overdose and my rapidly diminishing grip over my addiction. My eyes looked so sad.

I knew I had a problem but was in no way ready to stop. Before I had time to process these scary feelings, I quickly told myself a new story—I simply did too much. Next time, I would do less. Once I bought into my own narrative, I concluded the solution would be to search tirelessly to find a way to use just enough so I didn't get out of control again.

It's nothing a little cover-up can't fix, I told myself.

The next day I traveled to Staten Island via train and ferry. The little baggie of leftover cocaine from the night before was in a small pill bottle shoved deep into my suitcase. Does this sound insane to you? Well, welcome to the world of addiction. This moment, one where I seemingly should have stopped using drugs forever, is the perfect example of what addiction looks like. No amount of intellect, willpower, or scary near-death experiences will stop us unless we are spiritually ready. Emotionally dead. Mentally desperate. The part of our brain that controls these faculties, the prefrontal cortex, is the first to come offline in addiction. So, like a classic addict, I rode the escalator up to the ticket booth, where police officers with drug-sniffing canines were to my right and left. I had no idea they had that kind of security for the Staten Island ferry. My heart almost exploded out of my chest—*this is it*, I thought. *The jig is up.* I don't know why I was spared from arrest at that moment, but somehow, I walked right by and got on the boat.

My nerves were fried by the time I got to Staten Island, and when I hugged my sister hello, I shot her a look of deep concern. We needed to talk. We went upstairs and I told her everything. It felt so good to get it out. She stayed calm and told me exactly what I wanted to hear.

"It sounds like you just did too much, Sammy. Let me help you," she said.

She took the bag of leftover cocaine, scooped some on her pinky fingernail, and held it up for me. I readily sniffed it. She also took a bump, and we went back downstairs for the Christmas Eve festivities with her in-laws.

When I met up with Ryan the next day, I said nothing about the incident.

There had been so much lying and cheating up until this point that if he knew how bad my problem really was, he would leave me. I was certain that he was the only good thing left in my life, so I shoved my secret down deep. It was excruciating to hide it from him—he was the one I laid my head down on at the end of the day, my best friend, my partner. I quietly made a new game plan to stop doing cocaine and just get back to regular old drinking.

A few months into this attempt, I was out with some old childhood friends, the kind of people you don't see in three years but when you reunite, they feel like home. I noticed their facial expressions shift in that old familiar way and I softly inquired if they were doing cocaine. They winked, and like a puppy, I followed them into another dirty bathroom stall to snort some lines. Shame and self-loathing washed over me. In that moment, it became clear I couldn't stay away from cocaine if I was drinking alcohol. I proceeded to spend the next year switching uppers for downers, relying solely on my father for a constant supply of Xanax and Ambien to help me numb out at night. Ryan and I also smoked a lot of weed, and when I combined that with the prescription pills, it was blackout heaven. I didn't remember what I said and more important, I didn't remember how I felt.

Ryan would bring things up from the night before, and having no recollection, I would nod my head furiously as if I remembered it all. I learned how to cope with my addiction by denying what was painfully true—that my incredible ability to control my world had collapsed. Recognizing that truth meant the dissolution of who I was and a radical acceptance that I would have to become someone new. It also meant the very likely reality that the one person who loved me would leave me. None of that seemed possible to me, so I kept my dirty secret to myself for a good while longer.

I had been hiding my prescription pill bottle discreetly on the top shelf in our bathroom inside a dirty can filled with peripheral junk. I would turn the shower on, let the bathroom steam up, and lock the door behind me as I quickly twisted the pill bottle open and swallowed whatever concoction of pills I desired for the evening.

One day, for a reason I cannot explain, I decided to move the pill bottle into our sock drawer in the bedroom. Call this what you want—a God shot, a cry for help, or maybe just a sloppy decision by an addict who was deep in her disease. The next night, Ryan grabbed a pair of socks and pulled out the bottle. He looked at me, his eyes deep with disdain.

"You're still taking this shit?" he asked, disgusted.

There was nothing left to say. I had run out of lies and I was a healthy mix of tired and ashamed. I tried to blame my father. After all, he was the grown-up who was supplying me with the pills. But Ryan shook his head side to side as if to say, *You're fucking pathetic*. It was as though he'd tried to trust me one last time, and that discovery broke the final strand of hope that lived inside him. His look told me a few things. One, that I definitely had a problem. Two, that my shame was growing by the second. And three, if I didn't do something differently right away, he was gone.

I called Charlie, the only sober person I knew in my life. He had grown up in Hell's Kitchen when it wasn't trendy, when the streets were filled with gangsters and violence. His father was one of the last of the Irish mobsters. When he was thirteen, Charlie opened the front door to the man who shot and killed his dad. By the time we met, he was twenty-two years sober from heroin, and the light in his eyes could blind you. Despite his dark path, he lit up every room he entered, extending his hand to newcomers and old-timers alike. He smoked cigarettes like a chimney and his hands shook when he held them out, but he seemed to have made it to the other side of hell.

I didn't trust anyone at all, and the word "God" made me

want to puke, but I trusted Charlie. Considering a story like his, I had to believe that sobriety worked, even if I didn't think it could work for me. If it wasn't for Charlie's bright spirit, I'm not sure I would've ever made it into the recovery rooms of AA. He dragged me to many different meetings around the city. He listened intently to people's stories and often made a low, compassionate "hmm" in response, as if to say, "I really get that."

After six months sober, I went on vacation with Ryan to Turks and Caicos, a place we had frequented in my drinking days. Though I was technically sober, I wasn't working the Twelve Steps. They infuriated me, so I fought them—making me an addict without her medicine. My inner critic went apeshit as soon as we landed.

You look so fat in this bathing suit. I bet you wish you could have that fruity alcoholic drink you used to get here—it sounds so good. There's the weed guy. Fuck. Ugh, you need to lose five more pounds. Your thighs look huge. Whatever you do, do not say anything to Ryan about having a hard time right now because you've already fucked everything up and you're not about to ruin his vacation.

On and on and on my mind went. I literally drove myself insane for those few days, writhing in self-pity and obsessing over things I truly believed I could control if I just tried hard enough. My mind was a dangerous war zone, creating shame, doubt, and a massacre of hope everywhere I went.

When we got back to New York, I went to an AA meeting. Charlie nudged me to raise my hand and share my big, scary feelings. I shot my hand up despite my crippling anxiety. The exhaustion of carrying around that mental load for a week spewed out in the form of verbal diarrhea and heavy sobs. There, in the dank church off Forty-Second Street and Eighth Avenue, I finally realized what living sober without working the Twelve Steps looks like—mental obsession, brutal self-talk, and a death-grip on the people, places, and things around me.

It finally became clear to me exactly why I drank and used—who the hell would want to spend any time in a mind and body that was never good enough? This was the first moment of many in my recovery where the idea of giving my will or my life to some power I couldn't see felt like a good idea. I realized there might be another way of living besides punishing and white-knuckling my way through it all.

I didn't know of a God I could see or trust, and I didn't know how to turn my will over to it, but I knew this kind of thinking was unsustainable. Not because I suddenly believed in God, but because I believed that the inner critic between my ears would kill me—and I wasn't ready to die.

AN ALTERNATE LOOK AT STEP THREE

Let's talk about Step Three in real life. Here's the scenario: My sister is using drugs, and she knows that I know. She respects my sobriety and sees my life as something unattainable for her and something she doesn't believe she deserves. She often says things like, "I wish I could do what you're doing, Sammy. You're so amazing."

In moments like these, I feel my insides frantically spinning, the controller revving up to figure out exactly what to say to get her sober. Here is a peek at a typical pre–Step Three reaction I might have had, and then a post–Step Three reaction.

Reaction 1: There Isn't a Higher Power in Sight

Without God, here is what happens. During a phone call, I start by calmly telling my sister how good life can be sober. What begins as an honest depiction of the big, beautiful life I've built quickly becomes a sermon. I tell her about all the meetings nearby, how to ask for a sponsor, acknowledge the resistance she might feel doing the Steps and how much better her life will be after she does them. She listens silently, and after I'm done preaching, she quickly says, "Sorry, Sammy, I love you, but I have to go." Before she hangs up, I say, "Wait!"

I try to reason with her, asking if she hears what I am saying. As my temper escalates, she dismisses my concerns.

I yell into the phone, "What is the matter with you! Don't you see what you're doing? This is going to kill you!"

"I can't do this right now," she says calmly. Then she hangs up.

I am exhausted, infuriated, and powerless. And without God, I wake up and try the same thing all over again.

Reaction 2: Surrender (or Be Dragged)

When my sister expresses envy over the life I've built, I pause. I know that deep in her bones she is admitting she is an addict, but until she is ready to ask for help there is nothing I can do. I want to play God so badly. I want to say and do just the right thing to get her the help she needs. I want my sister to heal her trauma and know her worth. I want my sister back from the dead. Instead, I gently remind her that I am here if she ever wants my help. She thanks me, and the conversation diverts quickly into superficial things.

In the silence after we hang up, I feel the swirl of tsunami-level sensations rising inside me. I want so badly to get into action—I want to google how to stage an intervention, call my sister back and slap some sense into her, or figure out exactly the right thing to say or do to *fix* this. But as I sit in the quiet of this internal storm, I do nothing. I let the feelings rush to the surface. I let my belly heave and my voice crack as I sob uncontrollably. I am powerless over my sister's addiction, I feel insane trying to control it, and I am not her higher power.

These truths are painful to sit with, *doing* nothing. No matter how much I try to repair this damaged woman, I cannot. And since

I cannot repair it, I must grieve it. In moments like this, I long for the sister I want and need and may never have again.

In the quiet, I mourn the death of many generations before me, the women and mothers and grandmothers who placed themselves on the altar of martyrdom only to die as victims of their circumstances. Who swallowed pills to stop feeling their feelings. Who taught me that God is a liar, and if he can't stop the pain, drugs can. Who taught me that it is easier to self-medicate because the shame we carry is greater than our desire to heal.

In the solitude, I release myself of the duty of fixing and saving a woman I wish would be okay because I start to trust that no matter what, *I* will be okay. I let the tears fall as long as they need to, and though this exhausts me, I feel a little better when I'm done. My husband comes home and knows what kind of day I have had. We cuddle up on the couch and I let myself rest.

Wrap-Up: What Difference Did Surrender Make?

Let's talk through the first scenario. To start, I tried to exert power over someone and something I have absolutely no power over. Can I have power over her addiction? No. Is my life unmanageable when I try to control her addiction? Yes. In fact, my life feels out of control as I try desperately to get her sober. Do I feel insane by saying the same thing again and again and expecting different results? Yes. After all, I am an addict too, and no amount of external convincing ever got me sober. I know firsthand that it's an inside job.

Here is the transformative part of the work: While it may be true that her behavior is reckless, so is mine. In the first scenario, I am taking all my willpower and exerting it on this situation, hoping that if I say and do the exact right thing she will listen. I am anxious, irritated, and full of fear. I am resorting back to my hardwiring of having to "figure it all out," which is a place of deep comfort even when it's harmful.

As difficult as it is, my response in Reaction 2 is the one that will eventually lead to more peace. In the long run, what I am doing is bearing witness to my hardwiring, my ego, and my learned behaviors, but also realizing that they will hurt me if I rely on them in this situation.

I still let all the feelings come up—the fear, the anxiety, the grief. When I get through it, I reset my nervous system and use some new tools to get into a solution-focused frame of mind. Knowing there is a choice between suffering and surrendering is powerful; it gives me some freedom from the stranglehold of control.

The idea of taking whatever steps I can and then releasing the rest is so different from my natural state of fixing, managing, and manipulating. But after trying things a certain way so many times, I am tired of feeling awful and I have learned to become flexible. I have slowly practiced the art of asking for help, whether it is the literal kind I often need from my husband or the internal monologue kind: *Please help me make the decision that is for the highest good, even if it scares me to death*.

I am often asking my higher self for guidance—she is the God of my understanding. I am aware that my initial reaction is sometimes from a fear-based place, survival mode, the old, familiar hardwiring trying to direct my sail. I know now that when I start to feel anxious and obsessive, my self-will is in the driver's seat and my childhood patterns are taking over to try and protect me.

The practice of Step Three, then, is to recognize the old behaviors, remind ourselves we deserve to feel good, and then try a new response, thought, action, or behavior. This begins to cement new neural pathways and eventually, like training at the gym, this becomes a more automatic way of living. With enough practice, we can inherently know how to handle difficult situations without giving away our peace or our power.

STEP THREE: YOUR VERSION

When we get something out of our head and onto paper, we diffuse some of the power it has over us. The very act of writing down what we are willing to let go of is indeed the first step to surrendering that which we can no longer control. Let's get started.

1. Take out a piece of paper and write out your version of Step Three at the top: "[We] made a decision to turn our will and our lives over to the care of God as we understood Him [or Her or It]."[7]

2. Make it as personal and applicable to your life as you want. Pay special attention to the words "as we understood Him." Who or what is the "God" of your understanding? What does it look or feel like?

3. Once you've done that, list what you are already willing to share with a higher power. Maybe you are ready to release control of the results of an exam. Maybe you are ready to trust that your dating life has a different trajectory than the one you hoped for.

4. When you have your list, read each item over. Write down how it feels to tackle these things alone. Frustrating? Scary? Exhausting?

5. Last, write down how you want to feel. If you could trust that there was another way forward, what would you want

7 Alcoholics Anonymous World Services, *Twelve Steps and Twelve Traditions*, 34.

to experience? More faith? Less anxiety? More laughter? Better sleep?

Now you are clear about how you have been feeling versus how you want to feel. The goal is to recognize when you're in the old behaviors and disengage from them, regulate your nervous system, and commit to a tiny action that moves you closer to a new behavior. When you're done, go about your day and bear witness to how you feel. Become more conscious of when you want to control things and how that feels in your body. Come back to the work you just did and let it be a reminder that there is another way, and you are on the path to finding more peace.

4

INTERROGATING MY ANGER

AS I STRUNG TOGETHER SOME days and weeks sober, I felt the anger dripping out of dark corners, coming out as a snide comment or a passive-aggressive dig. Without the option to numb my feelings with a drink or a drug, my anger was a pretty heavy burden to bear. But what was I supposed to do with it?

I found out when I began the intense process of Step Four:

[We] made a searching and fearless moral inventory of ourselves.[8]

When I think of the word "inventory," I picture a business reviewing what is in stock, what is out, and what will be needed for the days and weeks ahead. The inventory process in Twelve Step programs is similar, but since it is a moral inventory, it requires a bit more excavation. In the formal Twelve Step process, Step Four requires you to draw four columns on a sheet of

---

8 Alcoholics Anonymous World Services, *Twelve Steps and Twelve Traditions* (New York: Alcoholics Anonymous World Services, 1981), 42.

paper. In the first column, you write down who or what you are mad at. In the second, you write what happened. In the third, you write what it affected. Was it your sense of safety? Self-worth? Financial security? And in the fourth column, you write down *your part* in the resentment.

Yep, that last column made me want to get up and leave, too. But before you slam the book closed, try to pause, trust the process, and keep reading.

When you are seething in anger, it is almost impossible to think of your role in the resentment. Neurobiologically this makes perfect sense. Cortisol is flooding your body and your sympathetic nervous system is on high alert. There is very little access to logic and reason. Once you have some time to cool off and regulate your nervous system, you can approach your resentments with a fresh perspective. I know these steps can seem irrelevant at first, but when you scan the people in your life who haven't processed their resentments versus the ones who have, the outcomes of their lives are often wildly different.

NOBODY PUSHES YOUR BUTTONS LIKE THE ONES WHO INSTALLED THEM

My family of origin is a prime example of what happens when anger has nowhere to go. Both my mother and my father never spent time unpacking their anger, so they either used it as a justification for their pain or pretended it didn't exist. I spent my life watching my mother blame others for all the bad things that happened to her, with absolutely no accountability for her actions.

As for my father, I used to joke that what belonged on his epitaph was "Never underestimate the power of denial." I have never known another person who could shove the truth so far down it literally disappeared from his consciousness. He would say something to me and when I inquired more, he would say, "I never said that." He had literally *just said it*. If I was persistent enough, he might acknowledge the truth for a second, but he quickly returned to a childlike state, changing the subject or making an inappropriate joke.

This was the beginning of feeling insane—gaslighting from my own flesh and blood. As a young girl, I watched my parents either emotionally implode or shut down, creating so much chaos and confusion in my home. There was screaming, yelling, crying, blaming, and avoiding. I didn't understand it at the time, but I now know that my parents' refusal to process their emotions either in a healthy way or at all led to a life with consistent dysfunction and only fleeting peace of mind.

When I started Step Four, I was not only clueless about processing my anger but also utterly stunned by the idea that I had any part to play in it. Despite my resistance, I kept hearing how important this step was to access a new sense of emotional freedom. As I chipped away at my anger, I uncovered many aspects of my personality that I subconsciously operated from without realizing it.

I started with my mother. She told me so much when I was young, and although at the time it made me feel close to her, I later felt betrayed by her honesty. First, she chose herself over her kids— every time she discharged her anger about our father on to us, it was now our burden to bear. Every time she swallowed her pills, I didn't know who she would become. This, of course, threatened my sense of safety in numerous ways. Not only was the fighting between them volatile and unpredictable, so were her moods. I felt responsible for managing her feelings and holding the family secrets.

As I thought about my fourth column, I felt an uprising inside me. How could I, as a small child, be responsible for anything my mother said or did? After all, children are helpless. They rely on their caregivers for emotional and physical safety, and they mold into whatever is required to stay alive and receive love. How, then, could any aspect of what my mother said or did when I was eight or ten or twelve be my fault? The short answer is, it can't—that's not what Step Four is about.

After doing the Twelve Steps dozens of times and spending many hours in therapy, I learned the difference between what a child and an adult are responsible for. On the one hand, I was thrust into a childhood with trauma, dysfunction, and a lack of boundaries, none of which I chose and none of which were my fault. On the other hand, I was now an adult who had an opportunity to reexamine my life and my resentments and become curious about them. From this space, I had a choice to either blame my mother or take ownership of what happened.

The fourth column is not meant to create blame or shame. Rather, it is meant to help us reimagine what we can do with our anger. For the first time in my life, I had a chance to see that my anger was keeping me stuck. By holding on to it, I couldn't fully forgive my mother, and I could continue to justify my addiction because of what I had lived through. Resentment, I heard in one of my earliest meetings, was like drinking poison and waiting for the other person to die. Much to my dismay, I had to befriend my anger. I needed to get curious about what my anger was trying to teach me. With open mindedness, I realized that the idea of loving my small self and forgiving my grown mother might actually set me free. Instead of giving my power away to the person who disappointed me, I could take it back and reshape my life. Anger is not the enemy many of us have been conditioned to believe it is.

That was one of my first moments of clarity brought on by Step Four. But as I trudged on, my resentments felt heavy and overwhelming. When I started to unpack my anger toward my father, I saw no possibility that I had a part to play. Not only was he emotionally absent throughout my bumpy adolescence, but he had also enabled my mother, my sister, and me in our addictions for as long as I could remember.

In hindsight, I saw his behavior as destructive and dangerous.

I felt devastated when I imagined my younger self, a girl who should have been protected by her father and who instead relied on him for drugs. Even as I chipped away at my resentment, I watched him relish in his codependency, which inevitably made me furious all over again.

Once, when I was visiting my sister and her children in New Jersey, my father drove there to hang out with us. I went upstairs to use the bathroom and heard my sister calling my father into the living room. I knew immediately that something shady was going on. After all, not that long ago, my father had supplied me with Xanax and Ambien whenever my heart desired. I came downstairs to see them in a sneaky exchange; when I shot them a judgmental look, they quickly scurried off.

"Are you giving her drugs, Dad?" I asked incredulously.

He backpedaled and denied it, but his eyes gave his guilt away.

"What the fuck is the matter with you, Dad! She's an addict, don't you get it? You're enabling her! That isn't love!" I berated him.

There were many instances when I tried to make him see that what he was doing was wrong; when I tried to control the narrative of my life. It seemed unbearable to admit that I had a father who provided drugs illegally to his own family. I couldn't accept that my father willingly kept his loved ones sick. I could not tolerate that my father was so spiritually limited that he didn't even see that his behavior was wrong.

My sponsor at the time posed a jarring question: "But when he was bringing *you* drugs, you didn't mind, did you?"

Shit. His words stung with truth. When I was in my active addiction, I loved that my father brought bottles of downers to help me after a long night of cocaine. He was someone I could count on and trust, a cosigner of my addiction before I was ready to stop, and someone who muted the shame. But now, as the fog cleared and I strung together some days sober, I was suddenly pissed about everything he did and didn't do. And now that I was ready to confront my demons and take responsibility for the damage I caused, I expected him to do the same.

Once again, as I approached my fourth column of Step Four, I uncovered that my resentment toward my father was tinged with self-centeredness and naivete. Self-centeredness because I wanted what I wanted when I wanted it, and naivete because I did not yet grasp the notion of addiction as a long-standing, familial sickness.

Much like me, my father confused enablement with love and derived a huge sense of self-worth from being the guy who could always get his people what they needed. I started to see my father as a human being, a deeply flawed man who loved me but had his own cross to bear. That doesn't mean I suddenly forgave him—that would come many years later—but my awareness of my resentment gave birth to a new perspective. Rather than seeing my father as an enemy, I saw him as a person who did his best with the very limited tools he had. I began to see that I could either continue to paint my father as the villain in my life story, or I could practice the art of forgiveness and compassion.

Getting this down on paper hurt like hell, but it helped me understand myself in a way that I was never taught. When I was a child, anger was modeled for me like this: When someone hurts you, it's their fault and you have permission to stew in your anger for as long as you'd like and use it as ammunition to justify all types of behavior.

Now, for the first time in my life, anger was reframed. Step Four rerouted my old beliefs and armed me with tools for everyday life—a method to control the madness of resentment when it inevitably strikes again. Rather than blame others or deny my feelings, I could now use my anger as a bridge toward curiosity. Is there an old behavioral pattern I have been stuck in? Am I engaging in toxic codependency? Self-entitlement? What lies underneath the anger?

Step Four gives us a conduit for our bodies to talk to our hearts. Resentment and anger often signal that something needs to be healed within, and if we look closely, we can find something inside us that we not only need to release but also have the power to change. And from this place, we can begin to experience a new kind of freedom.

AN ALTERNATE LOOK AT STEP FOUR

Let me dive into a fairly common experience. It's a new day and I resolve to be more positive and mindful. I leave the house feeling hopeful and refreshed on my way to work. Even though I'm starting to feel like I might need to change careers, just for today I commit to showing up at my office and doing my best. I am about to get on the freeway, someone cuts me off, and I instinctively honk (like a good New Yorker). They flip me off and I shout, "Fuck you, asshole!"

So much for positivity and mindfulness. This is not how I wanted to start the day. I take a deep breath, make it to work, and find a perfect parking spot out front. I grab my purse, walk around to the passenger side, and realize I forgot my computer in the car. I open the door and reach for it, but it slips out of my hand and falls into a puddle of water near the sidewalk. I rush inside and try to salvage it, laying out a towel and tipping the computer upside down. I quickly slurp my coffee, and it spills on my new white shirt. I am pissed and irritated, but I manage to get through the day. As a treat for handling all the bullshit, I decide to order food that night instead of cooking. I go to bed early but wake up at 2:00 a.m. with food poisoning.

Murphy's Law is so real sometimes, right? It can also spiral us right out. Let's look at some possible versions of events with and without Step Four in mind.

Reaction 1: The World Is Conspiring against Me

As the days pass, I forget all about mindfulness because life is throwing me too many curveballs. I think about leaving my job, but that feels too overwhelming, so I push it aside for another time. As the year rolls on, my work life seems good on paper because I'm making more money, but I am more miserable than ever. The extra money affords me a nicer car and some money in savings, but I'm not even close to affording a home. I don't see a way out of my current life, so I just stay put. I think about my bad luck—there has been so much of it. My entire family are addicts, my mother is bipolar, my job sucks, and my friendships are superficial at best.

Reaction 2: Pausing, Assessing, and Recognizing the Old Narrative

Months into the job, I am so unhappy that I can't ignore it anymore. I am a walking billboard of resentment. Both my patience and my temper are short. I start journaling about it and decide to interrogate my anger.

As I do, I realize I'm mad because I'm not getting paid what I think I'm worth, and this is exacerbated by the reality that I'm not doing what I love. At the very bottom of the digging, I feel undervalued, afraid, and alone. I've stayed because I believe I have no other option. All this time, I have been turning away from my inner knowing because I learned at an early age to play it safe.

Once I realize this, I take several weeks to imagine the life I want to live. I don't make any sudden changes, but I carve out space to dream. I start to tell myself a new story—that there is hope and that change is available to me. If I am the star of my own movie, then I write the script. I may not control the ending, but I can control the actions I take and the beliefs I buy into. This practice of mindfully moving toward my inner knowing instead of turning away from it gives birth to the next chapter of not just my career, but my life. I am freer and more open to whatever the universe has in store for me. And most importantly, I feel better.

Wrap-Up: So, What Now?

As with so many things, two things can be true at once: We can be accountable for our actions and compassionate for our mistakes. We can have depressing thoughts and belly laughs. We can be good people who make bad choices.

I have found that AA tends to lean toward self-centeredness as the main problem at the heart of addiction and bad decision making. Al-Anon and another Twelve Step program called ACA (Adult Children of Alcoholics), however, lean the other way—toward self-forgiveness. Human beings are doing some of both at any given time. We are beating ourselves up and trying to have grace. We are judging others and trying to have meaningful connections. We are engaging in negative self-talk and trying to have gratitude. So, as we embark on this very important part of the spiritual journey, remember that you can mess up, make mistakes, and still move forward.

When it comes to writing out your resentments for the first time, I strongly suggest putting yourself at the top of the list. Let the rest of the columns stay empty if they have to, but trust that as you become more self-aware, you will come to find that you have some unresolved anger toward yourself. There is a delicate dance between taking full ownership of your behavior and beating yourself up. This inventory process digs up all the dirt from under the rug so we can see it, name it, and free ourselves from it. Shame gains a lot of power in the dark, and Step Four shines a huge light on it. Eventually, the brighter we become, the more it disappears.

STEP FOUR: YOUR VERSION

Okay, let's get clear on who or what you have a resentment toward, with your version of Step Four: "[We] made a searching and fearless moral inventory of ourselves."[9] Ready?

1. Make a list. Yes, it might be very long. *Put yourself at the top of the list.* This may seem odd at first, but I promise it will be worth it. Maybe your family members make the list, your ex, your therapist, or your mother-in-law. Go beyond that. Is there a place you resent? An institution? A public policy? Put it all down on paper.

2. Dig deeper. Get very specific about what each person, place, thing, or situation did to you. It doesn't matter if it seems trivial, write it down and get it out of your head.

3. Write down how each one makes you feel. Why are you angry about it? What got hurt? Your ego? Pride? Financial security? Self-esteem?

4. This is the hardest part. It's time to consider what part you may have played in the resentment. I know it's infuriating, particularly in a resentment where you were very obviously wronged. But maybe you are taking something personally that isn't about you. Maybe you are expecting perfection from someone who is deeply flawed. Whatever it is, stay open to the possibility that a part of how you are viewing the resentment is contributing to the anger.

There is no rush to Step Four; it's one of the most lengthy and difficult of the Twelve Steps. Work on it a little at a time. Know that there is freedom on the other side of it. Trust that the power

---

9   Alcoholics Anonymous World Services, *Twelve Steps and Twelve Traditions*, 42.

the anger holds over you will diminish when the resentment moves from inside of you (in your head) to outside of you (on paper).

If you never learned a healthy way to process your anger, this practice is the beginning of creating new circuitry around how the nervous system responds to a fight-or-flight situation. With some reflection, you will start to recognize the old patterns that no longer work and create a moment of pause between the trigger and the reaction. You can feel the pain, reflect, and then move forward differently because you've given your body time to regulate. From a calm place, you can examine your part in the resentment and make new choices about how you want to move forward. Now anger doesn't control you. Your body doesn't respond with cortisol and adrenaline coursing through it. Instead, you give yourself time to feel your feelings, regulate, reflect, and then respond.

5

OUR SECRETS KEEP US SICK

AT FIRST GLANCE, STEP FIVE sounds a lot like Step Four. Step Five states:

> [We] admitted to God, to ourselves, and to another human being the exact nature of our wrongs.[10]

Once we have made a moral inventory of the people, places, things, and institutions we're angry at, aren't we done? Unfortunately, that's only the first part of the deal. Writing down a moral inventory is a huge unearthing of our personal demons, but it is not enough. The next step is admitting our mistakes to a God of our own understanding, ourselves, and another human being. When we speak our truth out loud, we diffuse its power and acquire the kind of humility necessary to live a more honest life. This is the next step in the process of self-discovery and personal transformation.

---

10 Alcoholics Anonymous World Services, *Twelve Steps and Twelve Traditions* (New York: Alcoholics Anonymous World Services, 1981), 55.

Addicts are experts at secret-keeping, so this habit must be smashed. Non-addicts are quite good at telling themselves lies too. Step Five is the beginning of a new practice of rigorous honesty, which helps us feel more aligned with our values and integrity. The other very important part of admitting wrongs is that they lose their power over us. Once we realize that life goes on after we've made a mistake—that we're not excluded from love and connection—we feel lighter and more hopeful.

When we feel ashamed, however, we feel dirty inside. We feel like we deserve the bad things in our lives—the deprecating self-talk, the unhealthy food, and the toxic relationships. We have no sense of self-worth, and worst of all, we have no reason to do better. Our secrets keep us sick. But when we talk about our shame, we shrink its power. We realize that we are not bad people, but good people who made bad choices. In the presence of another loving and supportive person, we begin to trust that our behaviors don't make us less lovable. If anything, they make us more relatable because we are expressing our true humanity, flaws and all. By admitting our behaviors out loud, we are changing our neurological pathways out of shame-based thinking and into a place of worthiness.

SPEAK UP

As my sponsor Charlie and I trudged through my inventory, I started to say things out loud that I had sworn to keep to myself. My mother's affair. My father's enablement. My drug overdose. When he encouraged me to share the details of my resentments, I darted my eyes like a guilty child, hoping we could move on to the next part of the work. He chuckled, which helped lighten the weight of the shame. He knew I was afraid, and he eased me into the work by telling tales of his own heroin addiction, the many overdoses he survived but shouldn't have, and the bad and often destructive decisions he made along the way.

I didn't know it at the time, but he was saving my life, passing the baton of recovery down to me. His honesty created a bridge between him and I, two seemingly different people with the same feelings of guilt and shame. The more transparent he was, the more comfortable I became about sharing my deepest, darkest secrets. I finally told him that I kept my overdose a secret from Ryan. In his warm way, he normalized the experience as one that is incredibly common among addicts, reassuring me that I was in the right place and that it could and would get better if I continued to be honest.

He listened to my rants without judgment, and he loved me through my darkest moments. His compassion helped lift the shame. To stay open and honest about my sobriety, I eventually told Ryan the truth about my overdose. I told him how excruciating it was to keep it from him and how ashamed I was of how bad it got. I apologized for waiting so long and cried a lot as I let the secret leave my body and start to live on the outside of me. Of course, this was the very beginning of my Twelve Step deep dive, and there would be a formal amends process coming around the corner, but the truth did set a part of me free.

The first time I spoke out loud about my resentments, a few things happened. For starters, I felt relieved. Carrying around anger was the equivalent of carrying a bag of bricks on my back; I walked around compartmentalized, turning away from parts of myself that required my attention and fragmenting the foundation of healthy self-esteem. I also felt raw and vulnerable. For me to be honest, my guard had to come down, which was terrifying. That said, my openness allowed a more truthful interpretation of my resentments to show up.

When I told my sponsor about my resentment toward my mother, he asked me what it affected. That was easy—just about everything. My sense of safety, my ability to cope with big feelings, and my constant need to protect other people at the expense of my own well-being. When my sponsor asked me what my part in it was, I was stumped. After a moment, he lovingly suggested that I was not looking at my mother as a sick woman. I was forgetting that she was doing the best she could with the tools she had. I had let my resentment cloud any notion of forgiveness and compassion because it felt easier to be mad. Acknowledging that my mother is a human being who is deeply flawed, who made some bad choices and who also loves me, is way more difficult. It's grown up. It requires me to balance two truths at once: first, that she made a lot of destructive choices, and second, that she did the best she could.

This process went deeper as my sponsor and I explored my anger at my father. When I examined his role in the family dynamic, I interpreted his behavior as deeply codependent and downright dangerous. Rage became a feeling I had to reckon with, and it would be many years before surrender, acceptance, and forgiveness showed up when I was in my father's presence. To make a start, though, I tried to view him like a sick loved one, a person who, like an addict, couldn't control his behavior even if it had potentially fatal consequences.

Here's the catch: I had lived my entire life up until this point harboring these resentments. Now that I was sober, I could feel them all, and at some point, they just made me feel sick and stuck. The interactions with my parents were hostile, my short temper and sharp tongue chipping away at our chance for true connection. As I worked through Step Five, I learned that I had to hold two truths about my parents in the same hand:

1. Their behaviors and decisions were often damaging.
2. They truly did the best they could with the limited tools they had (and sometimes their best sucked).

Owning the fact that my parents were deeply flawed was painful but necessary. As a sober woman, I began to see that neither of them had a strong sense of self, let alone self-worth. With a more compassionate perspective, I started the long practice of acceptance for the healthy parents I wanted and never had. I practiced empathy toward the people they wanted, but didn't know how, to be. To be completely honest, these moments of compassion were fleeting and would take the rest of my life to sort out, but Step Five was the beginning of writing my own story rather than giving the pen to someone else.

AN ALTERNATE LOOK AT STEP FIVE

In the middle of my early sobriety, I meet up with a girlfriend for lunch and ask about her marriage. Like me, she has been with her husband for fifteen years. Deep into raising kids, she says she feels like she lost the connection she and her husband once had. They sleep in different beds and barely have sex. She tries to make time for date nights, but they never get scheduled. She needs help around the house but ends up handling all the invisible tasks herself. On the rare occasion her husband asks to be intimate, she's so stressed out that her desire is gone. Then she looks down and says softly, "I met someone at the gym."

Her eyes dart up, looking for my judgment. I say nothing.

"We exchanged numbers, met for coffee, and kissed."

Silence.

"I'm falling for him. What should I do? I hate that I'm lying but I love that I feel alive again. I realize that I have been somewhat dead inside, and now that I'm experiencing this, I don't know how to stop or what to do."

I wait a moment before I ask, "Do you want to leave your husband?"

She thinks hard.

"No, definitely not."

She decides that she can't disclose the relationship to her husband and avoids his attempts at intimacy and connection. She admits that she feels guilty, ashamed, and angry.

My girlfriend is not unique. It is a fairly common experience to feel connected to someone and then, slowly or quickly, drift apart. Oftentimes, the drift happens through microfractures—a slow chipping away of trust that degrades the integrity of the relationship over time; the turning away from our partners when they're stressed; the numbing out with television instead of engaging in open-hearted conversation.

And then, one day, something snaps. Instead of communicating how we feel and what we need, we lash out in any number of passive-aggressive (or plainly aggressive) ways. We end up fighting, getting resentful, and guarding up against future hurt. It can take years before we understand how deeply this pattern has been ingrained. Maybe we learned at an early age to get our validation from something or someone outside of us. Maybe the experience of yelling, defending, or denying is familiar to us because we saw our parents do it too. Though we are hardwired for connection, we have learned how to disconnect. We are very good at feeling better through quick fixes like sugar, shopping, television, alcohol, Instagram, sex, and so on. We find ourselves in adulthood having the coping skills of a child—we don't know what we need, when to speak up, and how to sit in the discomfort.

What, then, does this scenario look like without Step Five? What about with it? Let's look.

Reaction 1: Keep the Secret Safe

My girlfriend is clear as to why she initiated the affair, and although it makes her feel guilty and anxious, she continues to engage in it.

She knows it's wrong, but she also knows that telling her husband means the jig is up.

As the days and weeks go on, she pulls further away from her husband and the fighting between them escalates. To mitigate her guilt, she scrolls through his social media and sees if she can catch him in a lie. She yells at him in front of the kids and feels exhausted. Her sense of self-worth is in the toilet, so she craves the dopamine hit from the secret relationship even more. She feels stuck in a vicious cycle of lying, cheating, and shame.

Reaction 2: Open Pandora's Box

She is riddled with anxiety from existing in two places at once and decides to call a therapist. She admits her affair right away and begins to unpack all the factors that have led up to this moment. She realizes that it goes way back to her childhood and watching her mother stay in an unhappy marriage.

She learned that marriage is a place where a woman's personal desires come second to raising a family. She learned that marriage doesn't mean happiness, and she hasn't been happy for a long time. In an effort to rebel, she found solace and aliveness in the arms of someone new.

As she peels back the complicated layers of her life story, she begins to heal and disengages in the affair. She still doesn't have clarity about whether she will stay married, but she feels reconnected to herself and committed to finding peace.

Wrap-Up: Honesty Is the New Secret-Keeping

I have never met someone who keeps a secret because it feels good. Secrets are kept because we have learned to justify the behavior. Because we think we are alone in the shame of the experience. Because we believe that sharing our truth will lead to rejection. Only after the oppression of keeping the secret is too suffocating do we consider sharing it. Only when we believe we are still lovable despite our worst behaviors do we acquire a readiness to release them. Telling the truth is brave as all hell—in a world that tells us to make things look shiny on the outside, living authentically is an act of revolution.

If you grew up in a home where secrets were revered, expect this part of the process to be difficult. When hiding the family secrets or repressing your feelings kept you safe, telling the truth might feel dangerous. This is a typical response from the nervous system—remember, it thrives off what it knows. The feedback loops for secret-keeping might be very strong, so it will take time, patience, and courage to disentangle from them.

I know it's hard, but it is our job as adults to recognize when these old patterns are no longer useful. What once helped with our safety and survival now keeps us trapped in a cycle of dysfunction. To change, we must reckon with the fear and discomfort of trying something new—something that used to threaten our very existence. Hopefully, we arrive at a place where the fear of being honest becomes less scary than living a lie.

STEP FIVE: YOUR VERSION

Now it's your turn to practice Step Five. As a reminder, Step Five is admitting to God, to ourselves, and to another human being the exact nature of our wrongs.[11] Time to get your journal.

1. Pull out the list you made from Step Four.
2. Say a prayer to absolutely anyone or anything, and ask the universe to listen to you as you read your list out loud.

---

11 Alcoholics Anonymous World Services, *Twelve Steps and Twelve Traditions*, 55.

3. After you read each resentment, take a moment to pause. Notice how you feel. The hope is that some of the grip the anger had over you loosens, but if not, that's okay too. Keep going.

4. When you have finished reading your entire list out loud, open to a blank page in your journal and start writing. Do not censor yourself or edit the language. Set a timer for five minutes and just let whatever wants to come out, come out.

5. Finally, write down one or two people you feel comfortable sharing your list with. I know! This is the scariest part. This is where shame wants to tell you to run in the other direction. (If you can't think of someone who makes you feel safe, I highly recommend a therapist—an objective bystander who can provide a safe space for you to share what's in your heart.)

As new resentments pop up—because they will—the practice is to dissect them, own them, and disclose them to someone else. These behaviors are meant to liberate us, not punish us. Remember, when we hold on to our anger, we give our power away. We are controlled by what happened to us. Now we know there is another way. When we investigate our anger and get curious about what we have done to contribute to it, we begin to take our power back. We begin to regain control in the only way we can—over our own lives.

6

I'M ACTING LIKE AN ASSHOLE—HELP!

HERE WE ARE, GOING ABOUT the business of living after admitting our deepest, darkest secrets. On the one hand, it's incredibly liberating. On the other, it's terrifying. It's a level of truth that once you see, you can't unsee. Unlike before, we now have a conscious awareness of our traumas, triggers, and tendencies. We realize that relying on old coping mechanisms has detrimental effects on our relationships and our well-being. We know that harboring resentments diminishes our ability to be present and joyful. What that entails, then, is vigilance about our words and actions, and a consistent willingness to surrender our old ideas to something beyond our primal reactions and our hardwiring. Whew.

It's time for Step Six:

> **[We] were entirely ready to have God remove
> all these defects of character.**[12]

---

12 Alcoholics Anonymous World Services, *Twelve Steps and Twelve Traditions* (New York: Alcoholics Anonymous World Services, 1981), 63.

This step is suggesting that we cultivate a readiness to turn old behavioral patterns into new ones. It is an offering to a power greater than us (whatever that may be) to see the person, place, thing, or situation on our list from Step Four differently so that we can have a new experience. Essentially, it is an act of humility that says, "I don't always know what's right. Please show me the way that points me toward the highest good."

When we think of it that way, it's less daunting. Behaviors work until they don't, so once you've hit your head against the wall enough times, you become more willing to try a new behavior. Step Six, then, is the start of taking ownership of old and harmful behaviors so that you can practice newer, healthier ones.

WHY DOES GOD HAVE TO BE HERE AT ALL?

In early recovery, I lived in all my character defects. Yes, I had put the drinks and drugs down and therefore achieved physical sobriety, but I had no real *emotional* sobriety. Because I relied solely on my willpower and perfectionism, everything had to be highly controlled for me to feel safe. I white-knuckled my way through everything, often feeling obsessive and anxious until whatever situation I was navigating had come and gone.

There was no peace or surrender in between my ears. Still, despite my dangerous self-talk, I refused to work the Steps the way they were outlined. I had no idea how I would ever come to terms with the word "God," but I also knew that I couldn't drink and use. What that looked like was a whole lot of misery—tons of physical triggers, endless emotional upheavals—a very sick woman who refused to take her medicine.

One thing I found continued solace in was Charlie's authenticity. I didn't believe in God, but I believed in him. My first year in recovery was brutal, the salivation on my tongue dripping every time I walked by a bar and heard people clink their margarita glasses together, the unrelenting voice in my head telling me I wasn't enough. Charlie pulled me from meeting to meeting, throwing his arm around me when he saw me struggle and cracking a smile.

"That's where I grew up," he said with a smirk as we walked past basketball courts in Hell's Kitchen. "Back when it was dangerous, not trendy."

Against all odds, this man was twenty-two years sober from heroin addiction. His bright blue eyes sparkled with optimism. He had a magnetic energy that was infused with the possibility of hope. I wanted the kind of freedom he seemed to have.

As I approached the end of my first year sober, I marveled at my abstinence, crediting much of the success to Charlie and his generosity. He took me through the Steps in quite a hurry, knowing damn well I didn't care for God and that if he didn't hold me close, I would duck and run. He became a sort of hero to me—a man who had seen so much and survived it all.

At this point, I was trudging my way through graduate school and got an opportunity to go to Los Angeles as a part of my clinical training. Charlie had started to seem a bit off—he was less predictable, his hands shook more often, and he wasn't quite as happy as he once was. I had no idea what was wrong, but I knew I didn't want to ruin the friendship by taking something personally that wasn't about me. So I decided to work with a temporary sponsor in LA and just go back to being Charlie's friend.

When I got to LA, I fell in love with the open sky and the warm air. The landscape was stunning, with beautiful mountains in one direction and sparkling beaches in another. I wanted to tell Charlie all the wonderful things I experienced, but every time I called, he didn't answer. I became resentful at the notion that my decision to find a new sponsor had pissed him off to the extent that he would ignore my calls—so much for not taking it personally! Finally, after several weeks of unanswered calls, his wife picked up.

"Sam, it's Holly. Charlie relapsed—that's why he hasn't been answering. It's not a good time right now but maybe you can see him when you get back to New York," she said. Click.

Relapsed!!! What?

It was incomprehensible to me that a man with the kind of recovery Charlie had could relapse. He was the pillar of AA—the one who showed us all that you can experience major trauma and overcome it. The one who showed us that life is worth living no matter how painful it gets. I couldn't wait to get home and see him in person—maybe I was missing something. I needed to hear his side of the story.

Three weeks later, I landed in New York and asked Charlie to meet up. He willingly agreed, and as I walked into the corner deli my stomach twisted in a knot. We looked into each other's eyes and I had a flashback to my childhood. His eyes were vacant, like my mother's, and I felt afraid.

"Charlie, what the fuck happened? Is it true? Did you relapse?"

My eyes begged him to tell me a lie. *Just tell me this is a practical joke, and we can go back to our banter and our meetings and our conversations on the stoop of a walk-up apartment.* He fidgeted with a sling he wore over his right shoulder.

"I got fucking shoulder surgery, and it messed me up. I got a staph infection and was in so much pain. They gave me Oxy. Holly's been up my ass, and I just want a fucking divorce," he mumbled.

I waited, but he said nothing more.

"Charlie—did you relapse or not? I don't understand!" I said, growing hot with rage and confusion.

He shook his head as if to say, "I don't know," and shrugged his shoulders. Desperate for company, he begged me to help him clean his apartment, since he couldn't use his right arm. As I tried wrapping my mind around the situation, the most stunning part of the interaction was that he was unrecognizable. It was as if someone had crawled their way behind his eyes and blew the light out.

This was not the first or last time I would be in the presence of a ghost—standing beside a person you love who is physically alive but spiritually dead.

We went to his midtown apartment, filled his laundry bag with dirty clothes, and hauled them to a local laundromat. He seemed so sad. I knew I was dealing with a shell of who he actually was, and it made me deeply uncomfortable. I decided I needed to take some space from him while he was in this state, though I still sent him loving messages when I could.

A couple of weeks later, I saw several missed calls from a sober girlfriend of mine. Lauren had become a fast friend in early recovery. She was nine years sober and for some reason took a liking to me, despite my attitude and disdain for AA.

"Sam, where are you? Are you sitting down?" Lauren asked when I finally answered.

I told her I was home, and she said she would meet me at my apartment—it was urgent. She came in the front door and as I tried to induce a laugh, her face dropped. She put her hand gently on my forearm and told me to sit down.

"Lauren, you're scaring me. What is it?" I pleaded.

"I'm so sorry, Sam. I'm just so sorry. Charlie's dead."

I looked at her. Stunned, I waited for her to tell me she was joking. When she didn't, the questions poured out of me.

"What? That can't be true. What happened? What do you mean?"

She paused, wiping a tear from her upper lip.

"He jumped out of his eighth-story window."

A visceral pain seared through me. I felt energy rise from my belly. I collapsed my head on Lauren's chest as we sobbed, two young women trying to process the enormous weight of the loss. Two young women suffering from addiction, trying to understand how someone who seemingly overcame their own is now dead. Two young women overwhelmed by grief.

The subsequent days and weeks were a blur, the sober community distraught at the news, everyone shaking their heads in disbelief that Charlie "fell" out of his eighth-story window onto Eighth Avenue. His inner circle—me included—knew that he jumped. We knew his addiction was alive and reinvigorated after his relapse and told him to end it all. We had to hold that gross truth in our hearts as the rest of the world saw it as an accident.

After that moment, I learned something I will never forget—addiction is out for blood. It does not discriminate. It doesn't care if you have fifty years sober or fifty days. If you slip, it can smell your vulnerability. It can hunt you down and ravage you and leave you for dead. If it could kill a guy like Charlie, it could definitely kill a girl like me. So I was left with a painful reality—to drink and use was to die.

But to me, believing in God was the equivalent of dismantling everything I had ever learned as a child about how to feel safe in the world.

My decision for the next four years of my life was to stay sober without a God of my own understanding. I had heard all the Steps professed many times from many speakers in the rooms of AA, but still God meant nothing. God had a forbidden feeling—it was only for the weak. The misguided. The suckers. My mother's explicit description of God lived on in my hardwiring as a survival mechanism, being of no use to people in real pain or struggle. God abandoned her when her mother called her fat and her father dropped dead of an aneurysm, and that God who hurt my mother lived on in my memory as a God I could never trust.

And yet, the program of recovery said we need a God to stay sober. I felt cursed, and yet I held on with a vigorous determination to stay sober without God. If anyone can do it, it's me. I didn't know it at the time, but it would take a bit longer before I would have the kind of readiness required to have a new spiritual experience. For now, I was ready to admit that I was an addict who couldn't drink or use because I was sure it would kill me like it did Charlie, but that was about all I could do.

AN ALTERNATE LOOK AT STEP SIX

After several years sober, I notice that I'm not eating as healthily as I used to or exercising regularly, which is not normal for me. As the year winds down, I vow to take better care of myself, joining the gym and meal prepping like a champ. But the first week into January, I receive a call that my mother has been hospitalized in an acute psych ward. As it turns out, the erratic behavior she had been exhibiting was mania, the part of bipolar disorder categorized by racing thoughts, reckless spending, and delusions of grandeur.

I rush over and find her asleep, heavily medicated on lithium to help stabilize her. The doctors tell me she will be okay so long as she takes the medication as prescribed. When she is discharged, she returns to her apartment and refuses to take her meds. I proceed to text and call constantly, urging her to be compliant so she remains safe. The more I ask, the louder she refuses. We fight often and I cry a lot. I skip the gym on most days because I'm exhausted, and I eat like shit because I'm sad.

Even with all the God-speak, let's look at how a couple of potential reactions might go without Step Six and then with it.

Reaction 1: I Will Rely on What I Learned as a Kid, No Matter What

I wake up each day and am too busy to eat, skipping breakfast, checking on Mom, and rushing off to work. I freeze my gym membership because I have no time to work out, and I eat whatever food is nearby in between responsibilities. At the end of the day, I stay up late because nighttime seems to be the only time that I have to myself. I fall asleep at 1:00 a.m. and the alarm clock goes off at 6:00 a.m. This becomes my new normal; I am exhausted, but I don't see a way out of this cycle.

Over the next several weeks, my mother continues to be manic, telling me about the next billionaire she is going to marry and the club she danced at all night until the sun came up. I am short-tempered and scared. When my friends ask if I'm okay, I say, "Not really, but what can I do?" They offer to help but I don't want to burden them.

Instead, I harden and decide that I just need to toughen up. I isolate myself more and feel angry and alone, riddled with self-pity at my life circumstances. I try to understand how I ended up here, playing the role of family caretaker despite vowing to take care of myself. I feel like life is playing a cruel joke on me and I'm pissed off. No matter how many times I try to reframe it, I feel like a victim, and I am filled with self-righteous anger.

Reaction 2: I Become Ready to Try a New Way

I call my closest friends over to my house and tell them what's going on. This inevitably leads to tears, and they graciously offer to help. I can feel my body tighten at the offer but I accept it anyway. We brainstorm on how everyone might play a small part to lighten the emotional load. One friend will bring me dinner tomorrow night, the other will call to check on me. This gives me a little bit of hope as I recalibrate how I want the next few days and weeks to look and feel.

I spend a little time grieving—for the plans I had for myself and for the mother I want but do not have—and then I promise not to abandon myself. I know how easy it would be to put all the focus outside of myself, please the people around me, and stew in anger.

After all, that's what I saw my mother do when I was growing up. She put her needs aside and then reveled in animosity even as it became a noose around her neck.

Although self-reliance is tempting, I know firsthand it doesn't lead to peace. All it does is temporarily make me feel in control of a situation that I am powerless over. The learned behavior gives me a false sense of power and then, when it fails to give me the desired outcome, I feel angry and disconnected. The new practice, then, is to accept the reality of the situation, ask for help, and turn inward. I make a promise to put the oxygen mask on myself first. Just for today, I can let myself feel all the painful feelings until I get to the other side—where hope and possibility live.

Wrap-Up: How to Turn a Liability into an Asset

Have you ever been stuck in a loop of anger that looks like this?

> You are stressed → you feel angry and disconnected →
> you lash out at your loved ones → you feel ashamed →
> you are more stressed → the cycle restarts again

If your answer is yes, let's start with a conscious decision to *get off* this merry-go-round. You have been on this ride many times before, and whenever you rely on this coping mechanism, you have less peace, laughter, serenity, and joy. Now, taking the work you have done on yourself up to this point, consider Step Six. Where in this situation are old behaviors and character traits getting in the way of your happiness? What are you willing to put down in exchange for more peace and power?

You may fail a thousand times, but you have to keep practicing. If you are truly done holding on to anger, control, or whatever character defect you identify with, then you are ready to practice new behaviors. With Step Six, the practice tweaks the cycle to look something like this:

> You notice an old behavior crop up → you ask whatever "god" you believe in to show you what to do next, as long as it is for the highest good → you ask your thoughts and behaviors to be directed toward something loving, tolerant, patient, and kind

Different, right? When we do this, we are not only building new feedback loops but also interrupting the old ones. As long as we continue to try, we can trust the scientific process that the practice of new behaviors will indeed create—and over time cement—new neurological patterns. We might find that we are living with less anger and more love. We might discover that life doesn't feel so hard so often, and when it does, we can sit with those feelings and then let them pass before engaging in an old behavior that we know isn't helpful.

Step Six is the start of something wonderful. After admitting our powerlessness, developing a new relationship with something other than our ego, and making an inventory of all our anger, pain, and fear, we arrive at a place where we are more ready than ever to release the aspects of ourselves that are contributing to our pain and suffering.

This work is slow and tedious. There are no quick fixes when we are trying to reprogram our nervous system. But remember, you build self-esteem by doing estimable acts. So every time you practice a new behavior, you are chipping away at the old wiring patterns that don't work for you anymore. You are performing an act of kindness to yourself because you know there is a better way, and you are willing to try. You are no longer talking about wanting a better life, you are *living* it. How cool is that? It may not be simple, but it's worth it, and so are you.

STEP SIX: YOUR VERSION

This process is a labor of love, but small habits yield big results over time. The simple act of doing this work slowly and consistently leaves less space for negative self-talk because we are literally cutting the neurological cords that have kept us stuck in anger, regret, guilt, and shame and creating pathways that help us access internal peace, serenity, joy, and freedom. Without further ado, let's work on Step Six: "[We] were entirely ready to have God remove all these defects of character."[13]

Here we go.

1. Make a list of some aspects about your character that you want to change—things you consider to be a "liability." Examples: rage, passive-aggressive behavior, self-centeredness, and defensiveness. As you write your list, acknowledge both sides of the coin—every liability has an equal and opposite asset.

2. For every character trait you want to change, draw a line next to it, and fill in how that same "liability" is an "asset."

3. Keep your list handy. (Maybe even hang it on your bathroom mirror as a reminder of what a beautiful, complicated human being you are!)

This is tough, so here is an example. Let's say you want to get rid of perfectionism because it is causing you pain, but it also makes you wildly productive. You might write:

Perfectionism (liability) → Ambitious, action
taker, highly successful (asset)

---

13 Alcoholics Anonymous World Services, *Twelve Steps and Twelve Traditions*, 63.

The next time perfectionism creeps in, invite compassion to the party. Perhaps you gently say to yourself, "It seems like I am worried about the outcome of this very important thing. I am trying to control it so that it goes perfectly, but I know that I can only control my actions and not the results. Thank you, ambition, you have done your job. I am going to relax now."

Do you see how Step Six is more than just saying to yourself, "Okay, God, whoever you are, I'm ready to have you remove all of my fucked-up parts." Instead, you are diving much deeper and getting rigorously honest—you know there are things about yourself that you want to change but they are also part of what makes you *you*. This practice is not about getting rid of any part of who you are but rather channeling the weaknesses in a specific direction until they become strengths.

7

DEAR GOD, IT'S TIME

AT FIRST GLANCE, STEP SEVEN seems eerily familiar:

[We] humbly asked Him to remove our shortcomings.[14]

We have already spent an extensive amount of time writing an inventory, admitting our wrongs, and conjuring up the readiness to have our most difficult character traits removed. What more could we do? Readiness is the step before the ask. Only after we become ready and willing to put down our tried-and-true coping mechanisms can we then ask for them to be removed.

When I first went through the Twelve Steps, these nuances were confusing and unclear, but over time I understood the subtleties as crucial elements in the process of spiritual transformation. If we are holding on tightly to coping mechanisms because they work for us, we will not want them (let alone ask for them) to be removed. If I use defensiveness as a way to guard

---

14 Alcoholics Anonymous World Services, *Twelve Steps and Twelve Traditions* (New York: Alcoholics Anonymous World Services, 1981), 70.

against heartbreak because everyone I have ever loved has left me, I will continue to use it until I feel so utterly desperate and alone that I am willing to try something new. When I am truly ready to release old thought patterns, I become open to asking for help, whether that be from a friend, family member, or divine essence. Once I ask, it's not as if a man with a white beard drops from the sky, grabs my character flaws, and pulls them away, never to be seen again.

But what if you, like me, still despise the word "God"? What if you, like me, haven't yet untangled the web of conditioned messages that told you God was punishing or God wasn't real? Believe it or not, that's normal and doesn't have to stop you from making a start.

The ask is an admittance, out loud, that you want to surrender your old habits and practice new ones. The ask is an act of humility that says, *I thought I knew how to handle this, but I realize I don't. Please help me.* The ask is merely the practice of a new coping mechanism, one that requires courage and vulnerability versus survival and defensiveness.

Simply put, the essence of Step Seven is humility. Can we ask a force greater than us—whether it's male, female, genderless, a feeling, a mantra, or an energetic force—to help us release the parts of ourselves that are keeping us stuck in anger, fear, envy, or resentment? Can we say, "Higher power, whoever or whatever you are, please help me redirect my thinking toward whatever is of the highest good"?

And if this is still too nuanced, you can try my personal favorite— surrender or be dragged. I can speak from personal experience: The emotional desperation from living within self-sabotaging behavior is unbearable. In these times, I was forced to finally surrender to a new way of thinking and acting. Was it terrifying? Yep. Was it worth it? Always.

WHAT EMOTIONAL ROCK BOTTOM LOOKS LIKE

The first few years of my marriage to Ryan were more painful than when we dated. New in recovery, I could finally see the layers of dysfunction that had piled up after all my years of cheating and lying. The fractures between us were evident and very painful. I would lean in for a kiss and he would turn his cheek away. Nights of initiating intimacy were met with one rejection after another and the explanation was always the same: "You're the one who cheated, Sam. You're the one who broke us."

As these days accumulated, I was filled with a gross combination of shame and rage. On the one hand, I was constantly confronted with the reality of what I had done during my addiction. On the other hand, Ryan had married me anyway. Yes, I had lied and cheated so many times I lost count. I had betrayed the very trust that was required to keep two people in a truly intimate relationship. But despite everything, he moved forward in the relationship so much that he married me, which clearly signaled a commitment to make this work despite our past. So, when I wasn't in the corner with my tail between my legs, my anger showed up. I wanted him to take responsibility for his part in staying and for the mess we were both left with to clean up.

Here we were, seemingly on the other side of the addiction, and he was pulling further away. The emotional withdrawal was excruciating, and I became more enraged every time he rejected me. As I tried to unpack the resentment, I wrote down everything he did (and didn't do) that hurt me. He rejected me physically and emotionally. He blamed me for his absence because I was the one who cheated. He didn't go to therapy. He didn't believe in Al-Anon. No matter what I said or did, it didn't change his mind. This affected just about everything.

"Why won't you work the Twelve Steps?! We can finally speak the same language and heal from everything that has happened," I'd plead.

Al-Anon, the sister program to AA, uses the Twelve Steps to help the loved ones who suffer on the other side of the addiction dynamic. I begged him regularly to either work a Twelve Step program, go to therapy, or both, only to be met with deep disdain.

"You're the one who did this, *not* me. It's not my job to fix it. *Stop* telling me what to do with my life," he'd say.

I spent the days and nights obsessing over how I could change his mind because my internal world felt so out of control. Yes, I was sober, but I didn't have a strong program. I had worked the Twelve Steps, but never formed a relationship with a higher power. I knew what my character defects were: perfectionism, people-pleasing, and self-centeredness, to name a few. And because I relied solely on myself to solve my problems, those character defects flared up regularly. My mom's voice rang firmly in my head: *The only person you can count on is yourself.*

I believed with every bone in my body that I could stay sober without God. The problem with that belief system is that I still needed things and people in the outside world to make me feel whole. For four years, I had successfully abstained from drugs and alcohol, but I had not cultivated an inner guidance system that I could trust and rely on.

The more Ryan emotionally withdrew from the relationship, the more unwound I became. I had put all my faith in my husband's love for me; without it, I felt like nothing and no one. And so I did what an unrecovered perfectionist would do—tried desperately to hold on to any ounce of control I could.

Unsurprisingly, as I pushed and pushed, he recoiled. The fighting between us escalated into daily outbursts of screaming and crying. The feeling of rage inside me was unfamiliar and scary. I had gotten to know my self-loathing voice quite well in recovery, but I had never experienced fury that made me want to turn violent until now.

"I'm going out of town again on Thursday," he said unapologetically one Tuesday night.

"But you just got back two days ago," I pointed out.

"And?" he responded.

When I was home alone later that week, I noticed his wedding ring in our jewelry box. I called and texted obsessively to ask him what the fuck was going on, and he didn't respond. My anger went from zero to one hundred so fast that I slammed my leg through our bedroom wall. I sobbed as I watched the paint chips fall to the ground—a painful reminder of my childhood and the constant chaos I found myself in. When Ryan got back from his trip, I confronted him head-on.

"I know you're cheating on me. Just tell me the truth!"

He was silent. I knew how to get his attention.

"Tell me the truth, you fucking pussy!"

He lurched forward and I felt his hot breath against my face as the tip of our noses touched.

"Don't you ever fucking call me a pussy again."

At that moment, I was once again face down in a very familiar pit. I had tried with all my might to control and manage my world so much and so often without any success that it had made me insane. The moment he got in my face was yet another rock bottom. It was the moment I watched my desire to control a world that felt deeply unstable blow up in my face. It was the moment I knew that despite my best efforts, I had to change what I was doing because it was slowly killing me.

Granted, I was not using drugs or alcohol, but I was certainly relying on my husband to make me feel good and whole inside. In that moment, I knew if I stayed in that house under those circumstances, I would die a slow spiritual death. And because I had seen it many times before, I also knew that a spiritual crisis left untreated could lead to relapse, which would also kill me. I already felt dead inside, but thankfully I had a will to live and a knowing that it had to be better than this. I didn't know where I was headed, but a tiny voice inside told me I had to leave this toxic environment, if only for a little while.

The journey of moving out was in fact a great journey inward. It began with a short stint on a mutual friend's couch nearby. After a weekend at her house, she told me she didn't want to be in the middle of our marriage and politely asked me to leave. Stunned and afraid, I called my sponsor Shannon. She lived in a sketchy neighborhood farther east, right near the freeway, but she had an empty bedroom for rent.

At first, this felt like a no-brainer. I packed a couple of suitcases and moved my things into her place. We hadn't worked together for very long, and it wasn't until I lived with her that I realized our ideas of working a program were completely opposite. I explained how insane my husband's behavior made me feel, and she pressed the idea of God on me like a plastic bag around a victim's head. She spent her days trying to convince me that God was the answer to all my problems, but I rejected the idea.

"That's *bullshit*! How is 'God' going to save my marriage? Ryan needs to tell me the fucking truth! Or at the very least he needs to get over what happened because it was so long ago!"

I'd run into my room and slam the door, a flashback to my teenage years when my mother and I had colossal fights that ended in banging doors and uncontrollable tears. A few weeks into this living situation, I came back to the house and noticed that all my things had been moved around in my room. I asked her if she went in there.

"Of course," she said. "It is my house, after all."

I was furious and decided to move, again, despite the deep fear of what all of this meant for my marriage and my life. I reached out to more sober girlfriends who put me in touch with a sober woman I didn't know. Her name was Danielle, and she had a cute one-bedroom apartment near the ocean. When we spoke, she said she was in a relationship and spent most nights with her boyfriend. When that was the case, I could sleep in her bed. When she slept at home, though, I would have to stay on an air mattress. The setup wasn't ideal, but the price was right, and my choices were limited, so I took it.

On the nights I had the apartment to myself, I struggled to function normally. It felt as though a dark cloud hovered over me everywhere I went. I ran on autopilot—eating takeout, exercising on the cheap elliptical in her kitchen, and binge-watching Netflix before bed. During the day, I went to work at my first job as a physical therapist and felt some reprieve in helping others. Though I could compartmentalize the emotional hell I was in, there was a growing financial fear inside of me as I realized I was truly on my own.

I had a doctorate in physical therapy, but I was making thirty-three dollars an hour. I started to pay close attention to the health-care industry and the patients' needs that weren't being met. Insurance covered a set number of sessions regardless of the diagnosis, after which they denied coverage. The entire health and wellness model was predicated on what the insurance companies were willing to pay, rather than what the patients needed. I started to wonder where these patients went after discharge and who they saw for continued care. I quickly realized it was the Pilates, yoga, and personal training instructors who were getting paid cash to improve their fitness and function. Shouldn't physical therapists do that? To fill that gap in the health-care market and meet my financial needs, I asked my patients if they were interested in working together on strength and conditioning for injury prevention. Most of them said yes, and I started training them at a local private gym. After a long workday, I'd return to the apartment and numb out with television and dessert.

Eventually, Danielle and her boyfriend broke up. I was now assigned to the air mattress in the living room, and somewhere in this transition I awoke in the middle of the night to her cat pissing on my leg. I shot up in bed, horrified. How was this my life? What was I doing here? Where was I going next? Shortly after, I had a trip planned to New York City to visit family. It was during that stay that I called Ryan, praying to something I didn't believe in that we could reconcile once and for all.

"I can't keep sleeping on other people's couches—I want to come back home," I pleaded, pacing back and forth in Union Square.

"I don't think we're ready yet. It just doesn't make sense," Ryan said.

"What the fuck, Ryan! I'm moving in and out of people's homes and you're deciding that we're not ready? Where am I supposed to go? We're married, for God's sake. This isn't fair!" I shouted, making a scene on the Manhattan street.

"I'm sorry. I don't know what to tell you."

He hung up as I stared at a mother happily pushing her baby in a stroller through the park.

I sat on a bench and dropped my head into my hands. After a heavy sob, I called a sober friend named Vanessa and proceeded to spew venomous words all over her about my shitty husband and my shitty life. I went on and on in an obsessive tirade, focusing once more on his behavior, words, and actions. She finally cut me off.

"Sam, here's the deal. You're not ready to leave your marriage, but your husband's not ready to have you move back in. You can't keep couch surfing because you're driving yourself insane. You need a sanctuary—a place to rest your head and heart. It's time to sign a lease and find a place that is yours so you can heal."

The idea that everything in my life as I knew it was coming undone felt unbearable. At the same time, my desire to control everyone and everything at all costs was truly harming me. It robbed me of my peace, my freedom, and my sanity. I'm not sure how I was able to do it, but I moved forward and found a place to call my own.

In my new apartment, I lay on the bare mattress and sobbed. I realized that without Ryan, I had no higher power. What I had was an empty program—the ability to abstain from drugs and alcohol using sheer willpower alone but with no peace of mind. It had become clear that substances could kill me, but my insides were distraught 24/7, which ultimately put me closer to a drink than I realized. I finally saw the dire necessity of working a Twelve Step program in its entirety, no shortcuts. Without a higher power, I became so self-reliant that all my character defects flared up until they drove me mad.

In this quiet space, I finally hit my true bottom. My bottom wasn't my overdose years before, the death of my sponsor, or the ongoing unmanageability of my life in early recovery. It was holding a mirror up to my soul and staring into empty eyes. This is the moment that people, until they live through it themselves, have a tough time understanding. In my sober and clinical experience, addicts and non-addicts alike cannot truly change until they are *spiritually* at the bottom.

For me, this was not obvious. Most people would assume the bottom is nearly dying from a cocaine overdose. In my case, I needed to exhaust every ounce of my resources before I could trust that there was another way forward. I had relied on the allure of control to the bitter end, and at five years sober it finally blew up in my face. I had hit the soul-level desperation that was required for real change to take place.

You might be wondering why my strong willpower couldn't save me from myself. If I was so strong-willed, couldn't I simply choose a new way to behave? There is a world in which people say we have the power to choose our own reality. In the land of self-help, there is often an idea that if only we choose differently, we can be happy. What this notion bypasses is the science of real change. It is simply not enough to one day decide to change your life, and then—*poof*—it's different. Why do you think so many people who lose large amounts of weight almost always gain it back? A quick decision leads to a quick (and temporary) outcome.

When it comes to rewiring the brain, our feedback loops have been strengthened through years of reinforcement. In my case, I was tightly wound around the idea that my willpower could solve all my problems—including my marital ones. I had worked those circuitries in every single way I knew how, and no matter how crazy it made me feel, I kept trying until I felt absolutely hopeless. Then and only then was I willing to see that the very feedback loops I had relied on my entire life were now putting my nervous system into unmanageable distress. Sending me to the brink of insanity. Pushing me toward relapse rather than recovery. Finally, the old circuitry wore out.

But it is merely a beginning to make a new choice. After that, the real work is in following the neural pathways all the way back to their origin and starting anew. A situation arises that creates fear. I begin to feel out of control. My nervous system revs up to do what it has always done to try and protect me. I have an awareness of where these pathways lead, and I don't react impulsively to the initial fight-or-flight response happening inside. I take a moment to practice a new thought, behavior, or action. I likely have a new outcome. There, in that moment, my brain is creating new synapses, which leads to the possibility of new outcomes and experiences.

AN ALTERNATE LOOK AT STEP SEVEN

When I am a year sober, I stomp my feet and demand that Ryan propose to me. He is right to hesitate, knowing of our shared challenges, but nevertheless he asks me to marry him. I joyfully say yes and start planning the wedding, dreaming of a future where we can finally be happy and healthy together.

A year into the marriage, though, I become resentful that Ryan wants to keep his finances separate from mine. Despite being together for seven years before the engagement, we never discussed our ideas of money in marriage. I had assumed we would share our lives in all the major realms—financial, emotional, and mental. Now that we're married, I learn that he feels the opposite. No matter how many ways I ask, Ryan wants to keep separate accounts. I reluctantly agree to this setup and have to ask him for money often because he makes more than I do. My spending is largely under his control, and it begins to piss me off. But the more I confront him, the more defensive he becomes.

You know the drill. Let's draw out some options for this scenario, first without the aid of Step Seven, followed by a path with a real-life application.

Reaction 1: All Bitter, No Sweet

This entire setup feels like a betrayal, and I feel bitter and hostile toward Ryan. I blame him for not sharing his finances with me, and the fighting between us is worsening. I am sure that if I convince him that this is what married people do, he will eventually agree. I spend my days and nights pleading my case. I think about my mother and her tales of when my father gambled away my inheritance. I resolve to change Ryan's mind. I will not let history repeat itself and be the victim of suffering and scarcity. I vow to protect a part of my heart because when I keep it open it always seems to end in disaster.

Reaction 2: Turning Inward and Upward

I walk around with anger and resentment, bitter at the circumstances and obsessive over how to change them. I can see how I want to manipulate my husband's thoughts and behaviors, and that when I do, he recoils more. This lack of control is infuriating but familiar, a place I end up when I try desperately to grasp for things that are out of my reach. As usual, this cycle leaves me feeling angry, exhausted, and afraid.

I think about control as my drug of choice, and how I want to get high off it. I know it is one of my main character defects, so I consider Step Seven and try to pray for my desire to control my world and the people in it to be removed. I admit that I am unhappy living this way and try to trust that there is a better way, even if I can't see or feel or touch it.

Rather than obsess over Ryan's behavior, I decide to turn the finger inward. What is his resistance triggering within me? Financial fear and emotional abandonment. What limiting beliefs do I have that are keeping me stuck in anger? That my mother was right—the only person I can count on is myself. What is my part in this resentment? I never had a discussion about finances before we got married. After taking my inventory, I move away from the problem and into the solution, brainstorming about how to earn extra income. I consider the pros and cons of outside help to discuss these harder topics. To the best of my ability, I practice kindness and patience as I honor all my big, scary feelings.

Wrap-Up: Rinse and Repeat (Then Do It Again)

This step is but a beginning. Many people are surprised to learn that after completing the Steps, they need to work them again, and again, and again. News flash! There is no graduation from your spiritual curriculum. The goal of living is not to figure it all out and be done with it. Life will continue to present situations we have never found ourselves in that take us to our knees, that challenge the old wiring patterns and force us to confront them. If we are lucky, these situations will require so much soul excavation that we will have no choice but to practice new ways of thinking, coping, and behaving. Step Seven is no different.

STEP SEVEN: YOUR VERSION

Practicing Step Seven is an ask: "[We] humbly asked Him to remove our shortcomings."[15]

This one is not a step-by-step activity or a detailed journaling of your past behavior or future desires. The way forward is through some kind of mantra or prayer that resonates with you, an offering up of an old thought pattern or behavior in exchange for seeing something in a new way. It is about recognizing behavior that is harmful and asking for guidance in having it removed.

As we remind ourselves that we would rather be *free* than *right*, we practice asking for a new perspective and a new attitude. We go out in the world and lift our heads up and try to assume the best of people. We stay open and loving toward what the world has to teach us. In recovery, there is something known as the Seventh Step Prayer, and it goes like this:

> My Creator, I am now willing that you should have all of me, good and bad. I pray that you now remove from me every single defect of character which stands in the way of my usefulness to you and my fellows. Grant me strength, as I go out from here, to do your bidding.

If writing things down is helpful, I challenge you to rewrite this prayer in a way that feels personal and relevant to you. Then, memorize and repeat it often, particularly when you feel an old behavior crop up.

Where you might normally control or manipulate, you instead pause and wait for divine inspiration. Where you might point the finger outward, you instead investigate what is being disrupted inside of you. Slowly, with consistent practice, our behaviors begin

15 Alcoholics Anonymous World Services, *Twelve Steps and Twelve Traditions*, 70.

to change. And inevitably, we will slip up again when some new situation creates a swirl of feelings like anger, jealousy, envy, regret, and resentment. We will be tempted to fall back on old ways of coping because they are so comfortable.

If we are steadfast, we won't engage in these subconscious behaviors quite as long the second, third, or fourth time around. If we're consistent and mindful, we might avoid old behaviors entirely and rely on a higher consciousness to direct our sail. Instead of blaming, we might run the scenario by a friend and get a fresh perspective. Instead of trying to fix a problem that is outside of our control, we might say a prayer and ask that our thoughts be redirected. As our new coping mechanisms become intrinsic, we start to rely on an internal guidance system that feels loving, kind, and gentle. We start to teach our nervous system that it can stand down—that we will be okay.

8

I'M SORRY

COMPARED TO SOME OF THE others, Step Eight seems relatively straightforward:

> [We] made a list of all persons we had harmed, and
> became willing to make amends to them all.[16]

The first part of this step is simple—grab the list of resentments from Step Four and transfer them to a new sheet of paper. This second part, though, calls into question a type of spiritual readiness that can be difficult to achieve. It asks us to become willing to say we're sorry. To look someone square in the eyes and own our mistakes. To consciously do better moving forward. Willingness calls the toughest emotions to the table—trust, faith, courage, and vulnerability.

For starters, it is an act of exquisite bravery to stand before someone and speak honestly about our greatest mistakes. It is also an act of humility to admit where we were wrong and how we plan

---

16 Alcoholics Anonymous World Services, *Twelve Steps and Twelve Traditions* (New York: Alcoholics Anonymous World Services, 1981), 77.

to change. It creates a level of accountability that is terrifying; now that we see our wrongs, it becomes increasingly difficult to deny them. What you finally see, you cannot unsee.

What complicates this more is when the person who hurt you should have loved and protected you, especially when you were young. It's one thing to apologize to a spouse who pissed you off, and it's another thing entirely to apologize to a parent who emotionally or physically abused you. I have done both, and they are equally hard for different reasons. But this is a "choose your hard" kind of moment. Of course it's hard to apologize when you've been mistreated. What is harder, in my experience, is hanging on to the anger and using it to justify old behavior that keeps you feeling small and stuck. If you're hesitant, I understand. As you are learning, my tendency is to only change when I absolutely have to—when the fear of whatever I want to do differently is less than the pain of my life as I know it.

THE NUANCE OF ACKNOWLEDGMENT

About five years into living in California, I was making breaded chicken in my one-bedroom apartment when my phone rang. It was a policeman in New York City.

"Mrs. Harte?" he asked sternly.

"Uh, yes," I stammered.

"I just wanted to let you know that we found your mother doing ballet outside of a Sephora in Times Square and she seems a bit out of it. We're going to bring her to the hospital now and she gave us your number so we could let you know." *What the actual fuck.*

"Oh my God, is she okay?" I asked worriedly.

"She's fine." Then he whispered just loud enough so I could hear, "I think she's manic."

Manic? As in manic-depressive? I was confused. The mother

I knew growing up was an untreated, self-medicated, clinically depressed woman, one whose tears I tried hard to catch and contain over many days and nights. But bipolar disorder was a different beast. I rummaged through my childhood memory bank and tried to find the missing pieces, the places where mania might have shown up and I mistook it for happiness. I recalled some major spending sprees when money was unusually abundant, for instance, ringing up more than a thousand dollars at the Gap, with me wondering who the hell we were. But everything seemed fuzzy around episodes of grandiosity and rapid excitability. The flood of images of my mother crying and yelling were so overwhelming.

"Where are you taking her?" I asked.

"To a psych ward here in the city called Bellevue. You can call later today and talk with the doctors," he replied. The officer hung up the phone and I was too numb to cry. I called my sister.

"Jess, you're not going to fucking believe this. Mom just got picked up by the police for acting crazy in the middle of Manhattan. What the hell do we do now?"

Disgusted and emotionally removed, she started the response with, "Figures." My sister had been estranged from my mother for a few years now, and I could feel her eyes roll through the phone.

We brainstormed and wondered whether we should call our father and let him know. They were still legally married, so the financial burden was on him. Emotionally, though, he would be as useful as a toddler trying to self-regulate after his parents suddenly turned off the television. We decided that we would wait for an update from the doctor at the psych ward and then reach out to our father with a plan.

A few hours later, I called and spoke to the head MD. He was terse, icy.

"Mrs. Harte, your mother is suffering from acute mania. We've stabilized her on a heavy dose of lithium, and she will need to leave here within forty-eight hours. Do you plan on picking her up?"

I listened, the pit in my belly growing.

"No, actually, I live in California. I don't understand. Are these the medications she will need to stay on forever? What if she stops taking them and becomes manic again? Should she even be living on her own?" I stammered through my questions, panicking.

"I'm sorry, Mrs. Harte, but we don't deal with aftercare. Please call back and let me know what you plan to do for discharge."

Click. The dial tone sounded like a siren in my ear. *What an asshole*, I thought. I called my sister back and told her that Mom would need a ride back to her place.

"Oh, hell no," she proclaimed. "I'm calling Dad."

We hung up and within thirty minutes I received a barrage of text messages from my father asking whether my mother used her insurance for this stay, how much it would cost, and what kind of medication she needed. As I watched the ellipses, I could feel my nervous system gearing up to try and manage the situation. *No*, I thought. *He's a grown man who chose to stay married to her. This is on him*. I didn't respond.

In the aftermath, I didn't know what to make of any of it. For starters, it was scary as hell. On top of that, I couldn't fix it or control it, but I sure did try.

"Mom, you're going to stay on your meds, right?" I'd plead.

"They make me feel terrible, Sam. Like the walking dead," she said resoundingly.

Within weeks after her discharge, I began to receive an onslaught of text messages that read something like this:

Sam, I was walking the boardwalk today and you wouldn't believe it—I met a man named Nick who owns hair salons all over Long Island and wants to make me the new manager of the one by my house. He wants to promote me to VP and then eventually take over his company. I'm going to be a millionaire, finally! I've walked about 20 miles today and I feel amazing . . . I haven't slept in 48 hours but I'm not even tired . . . I haven't felt this good in ages . . . aren't you happy for me? I'm finally happy.

There it was. Mania in full effect. A litany of messages filled with grandiosity and a kind of dopamine explosion that reminded me of my cocaine days. I wrote back anxiously.

Mom, I'm not sure this kind of happiness is real. I think your brain is telling you things that might not be true.

I waited with a knot in my throat.

I knew it! Even my own daughter who I raised with blood, sweat, and tears can't be happy for me . . . Why would you be? I'm finally happy and THIS is the response I get? You know what? I don't need you or your sister or this bullshit. If you don't want to hear about my life, then guess what? You won't anymore . . . Have a good life and leave me out of it . . . I'm going to go dancing now.

After this initial incident, there were four more. The final time was a week before I was scheduled to visit the East Coast and stay with my sister in New Jersey. My mother was more manic than ever and stayed awake for two days straight, riddled with excitement at the idea of seeing me again. At around noon in LA on a random Tuesday, my mother texted me incessantly asking where I was. Within minutes, my sister texted me too.

Sam, oh my god, mom is at the house and she's out of her mind. She thought you were in town today. She has been driving around on no sleep and told me she got lost on her way here. She sounds and looks crazy. Help!

I calmly wrote to my mother, saying that she had mixed up the dates and I wouldn't be in town until the following week. My sister took a secret video of my mom on her phone and sent it to me. My mother was speaking breathlessly, carrying bags of treats for the grandkids, and weighing no more than ninety-five pounds. My sister somehow convinced my mother to let a professional come and "check her out." Secretly, Jess called 911 and explained that her mother just showed up unannounced and mentally unstable, begging them to come right away and take her to a psych ward.

Jess watched as the EMTs carefully escorted my mother, her eyes filled with scorn, into the ambulance. To my mom, it was punishment—more evidence that my sister hated her. My sister called me, crying and terrified.

"Mom can't live on her own. She will literally get herself killed. We have to find a home for her, and Dad is going to have to get on board."

We called my father, whose response to the suggestion went something like, "A home? What? Those places are five thousand dollars and up! I can't afford that! Your mother will be fine. She will take her meds, and this will all work out. She's not even bipolar, she's just overreacting, as usual."

My sister and I raised hell.

"Dad, this is *not* the time to be in denial! This is mom's *fifth hospitalization* in the last three years! It's not our fault that you two are so entangled that the financial burden falls on you. You have to take responsibility for the choices you've made. This is what has to be done!" I shouted. I thought if I spoke louder, he would actually hear me.

My sister chimed in, calmly. "Dad, we need your help, okay? We will do this together. Sam is in California, so the first step is that we need to find an affordable place Mom can live, and then we need to clean out her apartment. I think she has dogs in there, too. This is going to suck, but we have no choice."

My father agreed begrudgingly, and we began to do some research.

We found an assisted living facility in Staten Island that had a broad range of clients—some with physical disabilities and sharp cognition, some with severe memory loss, and a few with mental illness. My father was careful not to mention that Mom was bipolar during the interview process. She was still taking the heavy dose of lithium from her most recent hospital stint and merely appeared tired to the normal person.

They accepted her with ease, and my father decided to save a few hundred dollars by not signing her up for assisted medication. She was totally capable of taking her daily dose, he convinced himself. Of course, he failed to mention that to my sister and me until we found out much later, when another manic episode nearly got her kicked out of the home.

Meanwhile, my sister and father had the brutal task of assessing and cleaning out my mother's apartment, a private guest house she had been living in for the past four years during all these manic episodes. I felt guilty and sad that I was three thousand miles away, but I also felt relieved that for once, the family drama wasn't collapsing on my shoulders. Jessica messaged me that morning: "Sam, I'm terrified. I wish you were here with me."

Jess took video footage of the living quarters as she and my dad attempted to clean it out. There was hardly any room to walk. The floor was covered in brand-new clothing, tags attached, in piles up to the ceiling, with small passageways to get from one place to another. There was dog poop everywhere, and once my sister made it into my mother's bedroom, she discovered not one, not two, but four small dogs roaming around, whining for food and water. Scraps of torn newspaper covered in dried urine littered the floor tiles. The bathtub had empty bottles of soap, splatters of shaving cream, and several cheap razors filled with clumps of hair and skin.

In the background of my sister's video, all I could hear was my father saying, "Oh God. Oh God." A momentary shattering of his denial in two tiny words. I wondered if God would save him now, or if my father would find a new magic trick to make his feelings disappear.

As you might imagine, experiences like these hardened me. I became less like a doormat and more like a shard of glass with both my parents—sharp and dangerous. My bitterness at their absolute inability to care for themselves made me furious. As much as I tried, I always had a chip on my shoulder in every interaction. With my father, this was daily, and with my mother, only when I decided to pick up the phone and talk. No matter how many times I told my father to stop mentioning Mom, he couldn't help himself.

"She's acting crazy! She's telling me that if I don't send her a certain amount of money a month, she will divorce me and take me for half of my worth!"

"You're acting like a child," I'd say, irritated. "I refuse to be in the middle of this drama."

My father was a New York City teacher and didn't have an estate to speak of; he was also a grown man who chose to stay in a toxic marriage where he was now financially entangled in my mother's life, which included her mental illness and the ramifications that had on her living situation. He couldn't stop babbling about his woes, never pausing to ask how I was doing or what I was feeling. It was maddening.

When I mustered up the courage to call my very sick mother, I couldn't get a word in edgewise. She ranted about her next multimillion-dollar venture and the many businessmen she had met who would make her rich. She'd describe her late nights at the club where she made the best of friends, dancing all night until the sun came up and rejecting men left and right.

"I'm so happy," she'd ramble.

"Mom, are you taking your meds?" I'd squeeze in the words between her frenetic bursts of energy.

"Sam, I've told you this a thousand times—the medication makes me feel like shit. I'm *happy*. Can't you see? Don't you want me to be happy? Why can't my own daughters be happy for me?"

I tried pausing and saying something gracious, but most of the time my response went something like, "Actually, Mom, what you think is happiness is *mania*. You can't see it because you're *in* it, but from the outside your behavior is erratic, irrational, and downright scary. I don't know how many times I can keep explaining this to you before you hear me."

After a wild emotional outburst, she would hang up on me, and I was left with deep anxiety and sorrow. And that was just it—my extreme hypervigilance from a lifetime of parents who acted like children left me feeling like an exposed nerve. Everything hurt. I wanted it to stop, and the default way I knew how to stop pain was to control things.

In this case, I was sure that if I just said the right thing to either my mom or dad, they would be struck sane—a radical moment of clarity zapping them out of their sickness. That, then, would be the beginning of a new relationship, one where I was seen and heard and protected. One where they were the adults, and I could stay the child. But no matter how many ways I said the same thing, I never got what I wanted. Instead, I collected one resentment after another for the parents I needed but never had. I spent years unable to accept their flaws, their deep humanity, their inability to keep me safe. But now I was a sober adult who had agency over her choices in a way that I never had as a child.

I stood at the precipice of a very difficult decision. Was I ready to make amends with my parents or did I want to hold on to my justifiable anger? This decision was extremely difficult because my coping skills, now harmful to me, were deeply ingrained. They had been formed over years and years of dysfunction as I tried to navigate an unstable world. There was *no* place in my upbringing where the practice of forgiveness was taught. In fact, what I learned as a child was that when someone hurts you, they can go fuck themselves into eternity. If someone did you dirty, they were sworn off forever. There was no grace, no ease, no amends. The readiness to remove these core beliefs, then, required a level of practice and courage that I had not yet faced.

As with the rest of the Steps, I came up against a wall of resistance as I approached Step Eight. It was infuriating to think of how I had harmed my parents, and for a while, it felt impossible to picture myself saying I was sorry for the way I treated them. But that's the thing about living in a sober and mindful way—without a drink or a drug to numb my experience in the world, I could feel the weight of my anger on my back. I could feel the exhaustion of my attempts at trying to control and manage my parents' behavior only to have it repeat itself again and again. I could recognize the insanity of telling a sick person to behave like a healthy person when they literally do not know how. Because these feelings were just under the surface of my skin—palpable, visceral—I needed a place to put them.

The Steps are a way to take ownership of your life so that you can access more peace and joy. I know how it feels to stay angry, and I am clear that there is no freedom down that road. If I wanted to set myself free, then I had to consider the ways I harmed my mother and father. Some behaviors I recognized were my rage, lack of patience, and endless attempts to control them. What Step Eight taught me is that if I stayed angry, I would keep my nervous system in a perpetual state of fight-or-flight. I would be making myself sick. I would be giving my power away by waiting for *them* to change so that *I* could feel better.

As I stayed sober, my threshold for emotional discomfort lowered, and I no longer wanted to walk around with a fuse of justifiable anger ready to blow. I wanted to feel free, peaceful even, in my own skin. I wanted my body to feel like a warm, cozy home. So I did what was suggested in recovery—I became willing to make amends, even to the people who hurt me the most. Especially to the people who I had a *right* to be angry with. My willingness was not a sign of weakness but the opposite—a fierce determination to set myself free, because that's what I knew I deserved.

Over the course of my sobriety, I made amends to my parents several times. To my father, I apologized for my short temper and persistent attitude. I thanked him for his constant support in my career endeavors. I expressed my desire to show up differently, from a more loving and forgiving place, when we were together.

To my mother, I apologized for how it must have felt to have her own daughters institutionalize her. Granted, I waited until she was stable so she could hear me, but I wanted to acknowledge the way she viewed it and then tell her that I did the best I could at the time. I wanted her to know that the decisions we made were because we loved and cared for her, and we were trying to protect her. I wanted her to know that we were afraid and that we acted out of love, despite what it may have felt like. I also apologized for the pain she felt when I pulled back emotionally, because I know she saw it as another piece of evidence in her story of abandonment. I let her know that I was doing some serious soul work at the time, and trying to communicate with her while she was unstable was too much for me to bear. It had nothing to do with my love for her. It had to do solely with the love I had cultivated for myself. I explained that it was one of the first times I had to be my own woman instead of my mother's daughter.

These conversations were very hard, but they lent themselves to some beautiful breakthroughs. Both my parents deeply appreciated what I said, and they even tried to imagine what it must have been like for me. It felt good to clear the air and talk to them as fellow humans who, like me, were just trying to figure out this thing called life. It felt comforting to be deeply honest about my own hurt and the hurt I caused them. It felt liberating to return to a place where I once again had access to power. Now that I knew I could become willing to make amends even in the worst of circumstances, I had a reference point for how to navigate other offenses, big and small, that would inevitably come.

If you take the most horrific thing that has ever happened to you—a deep betrayal, a molestation, an abandonment, years of gaslighting, childhood neglect or harm—and you confront it, what happens? If you let yourself go all the way into the feelings, what do you discover? There will likely be an onslaught of rage mixed with guilt, shame, blame, fear, defensiveness, and hostility. Noted.

Now what? What's the plan to discharge the feelings? Where should they go? They live in your body, in your cells, deep in your bones. You can reside there with them, letting them color the lens with which you see the world, or you can work to release them, so your body is truly your own.

Sometimes I ask myself a simple and poignant question: Do I want to be right, or do I want to be free? It is one of the more difficult tasks on a spiritual journey to forgive someone who has caused serious harm. It forces us to confront our deepest wounds, relive the trauma, grieve what was stolen from us, and welcome forgiveness and compassion into the picture. It requires us to let our guard down—the very thing we don't want to do because we had to put it up to survive those offenses. It demands that we practice vulnerability, what I now consider my superpower, and the continual opening of our heart when everything in our nervous system wants to shut it down.

Why? So we can make space for joy and compassion and love. Why? So we don't spend our one wild and precious life angry, bitter, and victimized. Why? So our life is worth living. So that we teach the generations after us to expand in the face of pain rather than contract, to try again and again so that the legacy we leave is about the unbelievable life we lived despite all that we've been through.

AN ALTERNATE LOOK AT STEP EIGHT

My best friend, who lives fifteen minutes away, calls and tells me she saw a house pop up on the market that looks perfect for her growing family. It even has an in-law suite attached that her mother-in-law can live in, and it's in a great part of town. She is also a few days away from birthing her second child. Prior to this, she has never mentioned moving to that part of town—she has only mentioned moving right where I live, which makes me happy because I believe we will be in each other's lives forever. I listen to her excitement and feel an anxious pit in my stomach. I wonder if I should say anything or just listen, but I remember that she constantly gives me unsolicited advice, so I don't think it's a big deal to chime in.

"This feels very impulsive," I say. "You're literally about to give birth, and I've never once heard you talk about living in that area."

Before I can say anything else, she interrupts and says sharply, "I don't like how you're speaking to me."

This leads to a big fight, one where I remind her that if she doesn't like hearing someone's unsolicited advice, then she should stop giving it out herself. We each defend our behavior and hang up the phone angry and upset.

Many of us have been here with the people we care about the most. Often, however, we don't follow up. We don't repair the rupture. But wouldn't it be so much better if we did?

Reaction 1: Scared, Angry, and Stubborn

I think about the conversation and realize that the idea of my best friend moving farther away hurts and scares me. It touches on my childhood abandonment wounds, triggering defensiveness and control. I realize that the young, anxiously attached girl inside of me is activated, but I feel justified in giving my opinion because my friend does that to me constantly. If she can dish it, then she should be able to take it. I steep in my anger and wait for her to reach out.

Reaction 2: Self-Reflective and Accountable

I get off the phone and let myself calm down because I know from experience that any response coming from a dysregulated state is not a good one. I go for a walk to clear my head and call a friend to run the scenario by her. I realize that I spoke from a place of fear and anxiety because I am afraid to lose my best friend. I also discover that I am accustomed to giving people advice because growing up in dysfunction taught me to put the focus outside of myself. I then get brutally honest about the moment before I interjected my opinion—I knew she didn't ask for my advice, but I said fuck it. Instead of self-regulating, I reacted.

In the aftermath of the fight, I realize that I don't want to be the kind of friend who dishes out unsolicited advice just because someone else does. I'd rather be the kind of friend who can manage their own anxiety and hold space for the people close to me to have their own experience. I realize that I want to stop fixing and saving the people I love and just start listening. I text her and tell her I'd like to talk when she is ready because I want to make amends.

Wrap-Up: Gentle Reminder

Remember, this is difficult, courageous work. You may very well feel like it's impossible to do this in real life, and that's okay. All you have to do is take a tiny step in a new direction and you've made a start. You can always choose to stay angry—but be clear that you get good at what you practice. By stewing in your resentments, you will keep your nervous system in a perpetual state of stress and dysregulation. By practicing forgiveness, you will be able to empathize with others, speak more kindly to yourself, and keep your heart open to new possibilities. Your nervous system will return to a resting state, making you open to what matters the most—deep connections and real love.

This is a practice of personal accountability in the face of crimes, big and small, against our humanity. It's hard, painful, and scary. But then I think of Charlie and my mother—two people who let anger get the best of them—and I know how that story ends. Without the willingness to forgive those who have hurt us the most, we see the world as a place that is out to get us, we guard up against future hurt, and we turn our backs on love, connection, and belonging.

STEP EIGHT: YOUR VERSION

It's time for you to get to work.

1. Take out your journal and either review the list from Step Four or simply write it again on a fresh piece of paper.

2. Consider each person on your list. Are you willing to make amends to them all? If not, how come?

3. When you feel blocked, write down your resistance. "They cheated on me." "They abused me." "They stole from me." Write it down and get it out of your body.

4. Set a timer for five minutes.

5. With your eyes closed, imagine that you are standing directly in front of your offender. They are defenseless, naked, grossly human. They can't hurt you. Picture them as a small child, before the world had its way with them. Find an image that helps your body settle, but let your rage and tears rise and release.

6. Look straight into their eyes and say, "I am willing to forgive you. I am so sad and hurt and angry, but I am willing to forgive you because I want more for my life than to be angry at you. I am willing to forgive you because I am worthy of a life free from this rage."

7. Place a hand over your heart. Try connecting to the feelings inside of you—don't try to change them or escape from them, just notice them as they come and go.

Take a big, beautiful breath. Just for today, you found a willingness to release your anger toward those who deserve it most. Just for today, you chose to do the hard work required to set yourself free. Congratulations. That's incredibly brave.

9

PURGATORY

THOUGH STEP NINE MAY SEEM brand new, in many ways it picks up the pieces of Step Four's aftermath. It says:

[We] made direct amends to such people [we had harmed] wherever possible, except when to do so would injure them or others.[17]

After sifting through the wreckage of our resentments, we discover our part in our anger. This is where we reclaim some power, because now we know what to change. Step Nine is the bridge back to life, allowing us to take the people on our inventory list and make direct amends to them because we understand what we did wrong. This, of course, must be done with discernment. There is great temptation when we do our first Fourth to rush around to all the people we have hurt and apologize profusely.

Though the intentions are good, this type of apology is rather empty-handed, as it isn't grounded in any true spiritual transformation. It is often the type of apology that is backed by intense shame

---

17 Alcoholics Anonymous World Services, *Twelve Steps and Twelve Traditions* (New York: Alcoholics Anonymous World Services, 1981), 83.

for past behaviors and is self-centered in nature because it is the offender who wants to feel resolved of their own guilt. When you arrive at Step Nine, however, you come from a neutral place, and you carefully assess whether the apology is going to be harmful or helpful before you open your mouth.

THE PAIN (AND BEAUTY) OF PROGRESS

The day I signed the lease and moved into my own apartment when Ryan and I were separated, I collapsed on a mattress on the floor, sobbing. Was I relieved to have a place? Yes. But I was also isolated, terrified, and in no shape to take care of myself. I wondered how I would fall asleep each night alone. No mind-altering substance, no husband, no faith. Just me.

I had to take care of myself, and though I'd been doing it since childhood, that was for survival. Now, I needed to introduce a new type of self-care, the kind that is grounded in a deep love and nurturing for one's own peace. As my idea of a higher power that was external to me collapsed, I was left with an emptiness that would either swallow me whole or birth something beautiful. With nothing and no one around, I sat in absolute silence and stillness for the first time in my life.

As I threw my body back onto the mattress, I wondered how I would fall asleep at night. When I was a little girl, my mother would stroke my hair to help me sleep. When I was a young woman, Ryan took over that task and ran his fingers through my hair every night until my eyes rolled back in my head. Now, as a grown woman alone in my bed, I shuddered at the idea of falling asleep alone. I realized that at thirty years old I had no idea how to soothe myself.

But then, in the darkness, gazing up at the high ceiling, I heard a whisper from within. *Why don't you put your arms around yourself.* The voice startled me. I had never heard it before. It felt calm and loving, and it seemed to rise up from my belly—different from my internal controller that ran amok between my ears when trying to problem-solve. Prior to this moment, most of the messages I received were frenetic and loud, heavily cerebral, and fueled with anxiety. Since this one was calm and clear, it caught my attention. I decided to listen to it. Awkward as it felt, I placed my palms flush against my ribs and hugged myself to sleep. Was this God? I had no idea. But if God could be anything I wanted and all I wanted was peace, then this felt like the closest thing to it.

And so began the long journey home to myself, one where love, kindness, and compassion were required. One where forgiveness and curiosity were practiced. I wept and I journaled. I prayed and I meditated. I made space to imagine a world in which I was free from the hardwired desire to control everything and everyone around me. I talked to myself, to the universe, to sober friends and family. I asked for guidance.

Every time I had the urge to call or send Ryan a message, I practiced a contrary action. Rather than dial his number, I called my sponsor or therapist. Rather than write the first thing on my mind, I paused and took a deep breath, buying myself a little more time to think things through. Instead of reaching for the short-term reward of trying to have my need for love and attention met by something outside of myself, I worked on the long-term gratification of small acts of self-love.

Slowly, I began to create an inner resilience that wasn't predicated on the world outside of me. In the early days of living on my own, I spent time dating myself. I took myself out to lunch, I went shopping, and I fell in love with yoga. I rediscovered how to play. I held myself when I was sad, and I explored myself when I was invigorated.

During this sacred time in my life, I started working with a new sponsor who was in both Al-Anon and AA. This was a life-changing decision. It put a brand-new spotlight on the Twelve Steps. Suddenly, instead of focusing the Steps on my relationship with drugs and alcohol, we zeroed in on the matter at hand—my marriage. I realized all the ways I was powerless over it, the insanity I felt trying to control it, and the dire need for a God of my own understanding to restore me to sanity. As we trudged along, we stopped at Step Nine, making amends, which I had practiced many times.

"Have you ever made amends to yourself?" my sponsor asked softly.

I halted. Not only had no one ever asked me that, but it had never even occurred to me as a possibility. This question was foreign to me largely because of my perfectionism. Growing up, when things didn't go according to my plan, I leveraged my self-criticism as a great motivator to keep myself in line. "You're so stupid," I'd say in the mirror.

I had also made up a story that kept the self-sabotaging narrative alive. Since I had cheated, I deserved what I got. I had let my guilt and shame over past actions cloud my judgment. I believed until that moment that I deserved Ryan's withdrawal, that the punishment fit the crime.

After spending six months working with this sponsor, I had a new perspective on my life. As the guilt and shame lifted, I realized that for the past two years I had either been romanticizing the past or fantasizing about the future. Through the practice of self-forgiveness, I could look the present reality squarely in the eye. And things weren't good or fair or right. The truth was that my marriage, and the growing disconnection between Ryan and me, was deeply unfulfilling. This radical question, then—had I ever forgiven myself?—was the moment my life changed. It was the ticket out of my deep suffering and the gateway to self-love.

During these months of deep self-reflection, Ryan and I started couples therapy. Finally, he was willing to work on the relationship. We seemed to be making progress, learning how to express our feelings without pointing fingers, and problem-solving when we hit a wall. As my lease neared termination, we decided we were ready to live together again. I was so relieved. Vindicated, even.

That's what was missing, I thought. *My own work. My own clearing of the shame that had kept me sick. Of course we're ready now.* I took my teal coffee table and linen tufted couch with me, and we merged lives again, only this time I came armed with a strong sense of self. A strong spirit and a tender heart. A strong awareness that whatever this issue was now, it was no longer about or because of me.

But even with all the transformative work I'd experienced, the problems persisted. I watched Ryan unravel. He still rebuffed my sexual advances, and the light in his eyes stayed out. I hadn't come back for this. I had done too much work to move backward. So, after eight months apart, I came out of my cage, stood in my square, and puffed up my chest.

"I don't want to do this anymore."

Ryan dropped to his knees and wailed like a dying animal, begging me to stay. My sweet intuition whispered, *Don't worry, you will find out everything you need to know.*

I resolved to stay for just a little bit longer.

A few weeks later, I was working with a client when my email pinged from a woman's name I didn't know. The email began, *I know you told me to leave you alone, but you have to help me get rid of him.* I opened it, and it was as long as a novel, flooded with photos and hotel receipts and loving exchanges that she and Ryan had shared over the years.

I dropped my phone in shock and quickly told my client I had an emergency. I called Ryan repeatedly until he picked up. I screamed and cursed and told him to *get the fuck out of my house and my life.* He begged me to meet him at home.

I unleashed my fury when we got there: "What is she talking about? When did I ever tell her to leave me alone? What have you done?!!!"

It all flooded out. Years earlier, when we were newly engaged, she had sent me a litany of emails with "no subject" in the title. I thought it was a virus and asked Ryan to check. He quickly said it was, and when I hopped in the shower, he responded to her from my email as if it were me. He wrote, "I know about the two of you, and we are working on our marriage, so please leave us alone." Ryan tried to forget about her and work on the marriage, but she was always there in the background, threatening to show up at our doorstep if he ended their relationship. Desperate to cover the lies, he visited her frequently, coming home and lying to my face. The unraveling I witnessed was evidence of his insanity, a failed attempt at living a double life. It was only when I wanted to leave the marriage for good that he finally ended things with her. And when he did, she kept her promise and told me everything.

Like a scene in a TV movie, I tossed Ryan's clothes outside and told him to move the fuck out. He did, but over the next two weeks, he would show up unannounced, leaving a memorial of photographs, concert tickets, and brochures that documented the last decade of our lives. I stood, once again, at the precipice of a hard decision: ramp up my controlling nature or surrender. Force him to leave me alone or pack my shit up and go. I told him he could have the house, tainted memories and all.

This time, I wasn't afraid. I found a great one-bedroom apartment in Brentwood and decorated it once again. Despite this being the most massive betrayal of my life, I finally knew the truth and decided I would never turn my back on my intuition again. Now sober and wholly embodying who I wanted to be, I did whatever I wanted. I smelled the skin of other men. I sucked the flesh of my desires. I made the bed wet with pleasure. I was heartbroken but also free. I felt my true nature return in a way I hadn't since childhood; I played and played to my heart's content.

It was glorious.

I drafted up the divorce papers and set the intention to leave this old place. Start new. Embrace my full humanity. My sexuality. My unknown future. As I roamed the streets of LA with a new sense of freedom, I cherished the love I had for myself and the inner knowing that everything that felt like it had been falling apart was only now coming together. I let my gut, my heart, and my head align and guide me.

And then came the whisper. My internal guide. She spoke softly.

I just want to know if you're done, she said. *Because if you are, it's okay. I will love and support you. But if you want to see what might be on the other side of this mess, you need to stay. So before you go, are you sure you're done?*

I sat quietly, waiting for the response to rise.

Fuck.

I wasn't done, and I wasn't ready to leave, and I was angry about it. I wanted to tell my intuition to change her mind and move on. I knew that to stay with Ryan and unpack our problems was to work. I knew that to stay was to go inward and excavate and forgive. I knew that to stay was to walk straight into the pain.

But I also knew that I was strong and brave and worthy of love. I knew that my mother's idea of forgiveness, the one I'd been taught so long ago, was limited and that I didn't want to wear her story on my back. I knew that I was walking straight into the fire willingly, mindfully, on my own terms. I knew the whisper of my own heart, and I couldn't turn my back on it again, no matter how many people shouted and told me to leave. So we went, her and I, the wise and the reinvented me, deep into the wilderness to rediscover the old and make it something new. We reentered the marriage carrying dichotomies: betrayal and forgiveness, calamity and serenity, fear and faith. All at the same time.

This was a terrifying period in my life, but it was also exhilarating. It felt like Ryan and I could finally have a fresh start and finally get to the other side of this big mess. My highest self could see that we were both good inside and that we had been terribly misguided by our upbringings, our hardwiring, and our life experiences.

The Steps had shown me again and again the power of practicing new behavior. The more consistently I practiced healthy habits, the more intrinsic they became. I prayed and meditated daily. I asked my higher power for guidance. I shared my triggers with Ryan and let him hold me. I often imagined him as a small boy who just wanted to be loved. My emotional sobriety was directly contingent on the rigor with which I worked the Twelve Steps, and they truly gave me a new lease on life. It was at this point that I realized the power they had to help all kinds of people through difficult situations, not just addicts.

Truth be told, no amount of practice will change who you are if you don't believe you are worth that practice. Not only did that process let me see my life with clarity and learn to love myself fully, but it also paved the way for me to forgive Ryan despite our rocky past. It paved the way to being rewired. It paved the way to happiness. Of every moment in my sobriety up until now, none was as important as making amends to myself.

AN ALTERNATE LOOK AT STEP NINE

While separated, I realize that I need to earn extra income. I still have my job at the physical therapy clinic, but I am also seeing private clients regularly. Most of them are former patients of mine, and we have a mutual care and respect for each other. I love being their strength and conditioning coach, and I love setting my own rates. A few months into this second job, though, my boss calls me into her office. "Samantha," she says, "it has come to my attention that you're stealing clients right out from under me. You're fired. Please gather your things and leave immediately."

I turn scarlet as shame corrodes my cells. My mind races, and I robotically place my belongings in a box. As I leave, panic floods my insides.

Reaction 1: Lose My Shit and Point a Finger

I feel a swirl of anxiety as I wonder what will happen next. I engage in a self-deprecating narrative that is as familiar as it is toxic. "Fucking idiot!" I shout. "Always have to do something stupid, don't you!" I throw a glass vase across the floor and spend the rest of the night beating myself up in between sobs. The next day, I feel a heavy sense of shame as l wonder how I am going to survive.

Reaction 2: Use the Tools Available

I leave the office and go home to my apartment, tears pouring down my face. I am embarrassed about my behavior and fearful of my financial situation. I can feel the inner critic revving up inside me, but I know that voice all too well. It's mean and unhelpful. Instead of engaging with it, I decide to call my sponsor and go to a meeting. After some time in self-reflection, I realize that although my need for financial stability is real, my boss has a right to feel threatened. I could spend the next several days and weeks beating myself up, or I could feel my feelings and get into the solution. I brainstorm about the different ways to earn money, and I trust that I have enough recovery to use this incident as an opportunity for growth, both personally and professionally.

Wrap-Up: How the Tables Have Turned

Before I got sober, I spoke to myself with great disdain. No matter how well I did on an exam, I could have studied harder. No matter how fit I was, I could have been thinner. It took years into sobriety to uncover the root of this negative self-talk and to rewire my brain to have a new internal dialogue.

When we make a mistake, our ego often chimes in to beat us up and tell us a story about how terribly things went. Because we are in fear, it wants to regain control by selling us a story that if we flog ourselves enough, we won't ever make the same mistake again. It barges in with nasty language to whip us into shape—you made a mistake, you're an idiot, you'd better not do that again—in an attempt to give us a false sense of security that we have learned our lesson for good. After sufficient laceration, we have an illusion that this mistake will never happen again. Our world can go back to being neat and tidy, a place within our control where we are safe. Not only is this untrue, because of course we will make more mistakes, but it is also dangerous.

It wasn't until I worked Step Nine with a new sponsor and in a new way that I finally had a new experience around forgiveness and compassion. What I discovered is that I had to learn how to forgive myself for my mistakes, feel the feelings of disappointment, and then have the resilience to keep trudging forward.

The practice of learning to forgive yourself and others is lifelong. One new behavior at a time, we can tell ourselves that we are good people that sometimes make bad choices. We can love ourselves through our mistakes, make amends by changing the behavior we are sorry for, and then go about the business of living. By practicing forgiveness, we not only create new neural pathways for how we treat ourselves; we also create a road map for how to treat others. There's a saying in recovery: You cannot transmit what you haven't got. If you cannot forgive yourself, then there's no way you can forgive others.

STEP NINE: YOUR VERSION

This step—"[We] made direct amends to such people wherever possible, except when to do so would injure them or others"[18]—can be particularly tricky.

Before you dig into it, let's use my story to talk about what it looks like to make direct amends. When it came to myself, I stood in front of the mirror. I looked straight into my own eyes—which, if you've never tried, you should—and said I was sorry. *I'm sorry for how hard I have been on you. I am sorry for the shame you've been carrying around. I know you were doing your best at the time, and believe it or not, you deserve to be happy. I love you.* Once I forgave myself, I could see my marriage for what it really was and decide, from a healed place, whether I wanted to stay in it or not.

Now let's consider "amends" that might injure a person. If I had shared with Ryan every single instance where I cheated or lied, that would most likely have unburdened me but heavily burdened him. At this point in our relationship, we were married and navigating a stormy period that no amount of past behavior could fix or change. So my amends to him were sincere and heartfelt but made with discernment. I apologized for my selfishness, my poor decisions, and my untrustworthy actions. I committed to treating both myself and him differently moving forward. To the best of my ability, I practiced kindness, compassion, and honest communication.

Now it's your turn.

1. Make a list of the people you have harmed, and *write your name down first.*
2. Put the list down and place your hands on your heart. Imagine the people you have hurt and look them directly

---

18 Alcoholics Anonymous World Services, *Twelve Steps and Twelve Traditions*, 83.

in the eye. What does it stir up in you? Spend three to five
minutes feeling all the feelings.

3. Write down what came up, and then write something kind
   about each person.

4. Create a plan for when and how you will make amends,
   assuming it will not be injurious to others. Pro tip: Cross-
   check your plan with a therapist or a friend you deeply trust.

This exercise begins the practice of a critical life skill—not the
kind you learn in school. It demands that you give forgiveness your
full attention. That you treat it as a necessity, as important as the
air you breathe. No matter how old you are, there will come a time
in your life where someone will hurt you (or you will hurt yourself). You will have a choice to make. Either get resentful and stew
in anger or feel your feelings and forgive. In my lived experience,
forgiveness has saved my life, time and time again. It restored my
sense of self-worth, my marriage, and my ability to live and love
more fully. I want the same for you.

10

MISHAPS

PEOPLE IN RECOVERY CONSIDER STEP Ten the bridge that transports us to the land of the living. In other words, we have hit bottom, admitted defeat, found a higher power, and made some serious amends. Our past no longer holds a noose around our neck, so we can begin living in the here and now. Step Ten goes like this:

> [We] continued to take personal inventory and when
> we were wrong promptly admitted it.[19]

The final three steps are, for lack of a better term, maintenance steps. Once we admit our powerlessness, find a power greater than ourselves, and sweep our secrets out from under the rug, we have theoretically stepped out of autopilot and into consciousness. Step Ten becomes a point of accountability—a place we can return to at the end of the day to see where we might have gone wrong, what we could have done better, and what we did well.

---

19 Alcoholics Anonymous World Services, *Twelve Steps and Twelve Traditions* (New York: Alcoholics Anonymous World Services, 1981), 88.

They say in recovery rooms that resentment is the number one offender—the thing that takes more addicts into a relapse than anything else. I disagree. *It is my experience, again and again, that shame is the number one offender.* When we behave in a way we are not proud of, and there is no way to clear the shame, it grows inside us like a fungus, infecting our thoughts, attitudes, and actions. It spreads like a parasite, telling us we're fine when we're not, we don't care when we do, and we're not worthy when we are. It is a breeding ground for discontent, rage, numbing, and relapse. It can, and will, kill you.

As much as we wish we could work the Twelve Steps and be done with it, the truth is that living a spiritual life has no end date. Step Ten is a practice of personal responsibility, guiding us to take ownership of our actions and admit our wrongs. It is a practice of humility, so that instead of walking around in self-righteous anger or self-pity, we can recognize our part, vow to do better, and move forward. If we want to continue to grow and rewire our nervous system so that productive thoughts and meaningful behaviors become intrinsic, we need to continue to practice. We need to do the work.

ONE MILLISECOND AT A TIME

My pregnancy journey began with a positive test after only the second month of trying for a baby. I was elated, especially after the stories my mom shared about her fertility struggles with my sister. Being the control freak that I am, I tested as soon as humanly possible with one of those early-detection test kits. Within a few days of the positive test, I went to the bathroom and saw blood on the toilet paper. It was bright red. I panicked, googled "bleeding in the first trimester," and read horror stories about women who had miscarried anywhere from week five all the way to week fourteen. I kept googling. More horror stories about women who had to deliver their dead babies at five, six, and seven months.

I called Ryan. He urged me to calm down and try to get an appointment with a doctor. My normal gynecologist was unavailable, so I talked to a nurse practitioner.

"It's too early to see anything on an ultrasound. Take it easy," she said. "If the bleeding worsens, you are likely having a miscarriage. It's early enough that your body will take care of everything on its own. No need to worry or come in."

We hung up. I started sobbing, feeling the blood coming out quickly now, hormones plunging. I called Ryan back and told him we had lost the baby. He stayed calm and tried to reassure me that it was a blessing in disguise and to look at the bright side—now we know we can get pregnant.

But all I could do was cry, having already imagined what it would feel like to hold and kiss and love this baby. All I could do was grieve my hopes and dreams and expectations, the birth story I wanted to write, the body I wished I had. I felt terribly alone in those next few days, walking around with my child falling out of me and the world marching on.

The way I coped was an old, familiar pattern. I became hypervigilant about my menstrual cycle and jumped on my husband the second I was in my ovulation window. There was nothing sexy about this time; sex was strictly business. *You will fuck me, I will get pregnant, and we will maximize our chances because I'll be damned if I don't get pregnant again right away.*

I seemed to have forgotten all about prayer and meditation, and any notion of God was a distant memory. Two months later, I was pregnant again. Riddled with anxiety that I would lose this baby too, I tried hard to stay present each day. I was very lucky the second time around, having virtually no problems—until labor began.

On the evening of June second, a searing pain shot across my abdomen in a place deep and unfamiliar.

"I just felt something brand new and super painful," I warned Ryan. "Not sure if it's labor, but we will see if it happens again."

As time went on, those pains increased in frequency and duration, followed by losing my mucus plug and failed attempts to sleep. At 3:00 a.m., I finally decided that I might as well eat something and shower. My vanilla almond granola came right up and out in the shower, and the contractions worsened with very little time between them. Ryan did his best to rub my hips and keep me calm, and when the contractions were less than two minutes apart, I told him to take me to the hospital.

I had been laboring nearly all night and assumed I would be at least five centimeters dilated. To my horror, I was barely one. I looked up at the nurse.

"Please don't send me home," I begged her.

"Oh no, we want to monitor you. Your contractions are too close together not to," she reassured me.

I got an epidural shortly after. The hours rolled on. When active labor started, my body convulsed for hours. I was tired but sure that my baby was coming soon. My doctor stopped in to check on me and felt my leg, saying it was very hot. I had a fever, and so did the baby. The nurses also thought I was bleeding more than I should be, and no one was sure if or when my water broke.

I was pumped with all types of fluids—IV antibiotics, saline solution, and an epidural. The saline was because my baby's heart rate kept dropping, and they wanted to see if the heart rate would stabilize when they added extra fluid. If it did, it would indicate the cord was around the baby's neck. By hour twenty-three, I hadn't slept at all, and I was only seven centimeters dilated. My doctor's concern level went from orange to red.

"We can give this a little more time to see if you get to ten centimeters, and if you don't it will be an emergency C-section, or we can go into surgery now, because this baby is in distress."

I looked at Ryan. For him, it was a no-brainer. For me, it went against every plan I had made for my labor and delivery (the irony of that sentence does not elude me). But the exhaustion and fear had peaked, and I just wanted what was best for my baby.

The anesthesiologist numbed me well, leaving the sensory nerves functioning only enough for me to feel the tickle of the scalpel across my lower abdomen. How strange, I thought, that I know my body is being cut open right now, my organs pushed aside, my baby pulled out, and yet it doesn't hurt. How strange to know that once the medicine wears off, it will hurt like hell, and I will also have a baby to keep alive.

"You're going to feel a lot of pressure," said the doctor. "Are you ready?"

What else could I say besides yes? I felt my entire body elevate off the operating table and crash back down.

"We need to do that one more time," they said.

I pictured my soft tissue being stretched and torn and traumatized as I nodded yes once again. One more time, my body lifted off the surgical table and as it came back down, I heard the cry.

"It's a boy!" everyone shouted. Ryan's eyes welled as he cut the umbilical cord and held his son for the first time. I was elated and drained beyond measure.

In the recovery room, the nurses put Jack on my chest, and we snuggled and slept together as my vitals stabilized. The next few days were hard as hell. I was three times my original size, in horrific pain, and desperately clinging to the notion that my son would receive breast milk and breast milk only. When he was whisked away to the NICU for unusually low oxygen levels, they gave him formula. I told the nurses to wake me in the middle of the night and wheel me in so I could breastfeed, and when they tried, my body convulsed as my temperature plunged. I couldn't get warm, but I kept trying. They covered me with many blankets, but I couldn't stop shaking.

"I know you want to see your baby, but your body needs to

rest. We will take good care of him," one of the nurses said, bending over me. I had no fight left and went back to bed. Fortunately, Jack was brought back to our room the next day.

By the time I got home, I was relieved to have made it. Nothing about the labor, delivery, and hospital stay was what I had imagined. I felt like I had been to war and was finally coming home. The first two weeks were blissful, me and baby and hubby in our sweet cocoon. After everything we had been through, we had arrived at this moment, one I had dreamed of my whole life.

And then the anxiety kicked in. Every sound and movement Jack made put my nervous system on high alert. I counted the minutes he slept, worried that he wasn't breathing, and feared he wasn't getting enough milk. He was what moms call a "catnapper," sleeping for only twenty minutes at a time, just long enough for me to clean up around the house and pump. By the time he woke up, I had no energy to care for him, but I picked him up and sang him songs and loved him the best I could. Friends would call and ask how I was, and I would say "great" between sobs.

It was odd that I couldn't stop crying, but I had read about the baby blues, and this seemed par for the course, especially after what I went through. Ryan and I came up with a clever plan for nighttime sleep. I, being the early riser, went to sleep around 9:00 p.m. and woke up at 2:00 a.m., at which point he went to bed, and I remained on mommy duty for the rest of the night. As the days went on, Jack slept for longer stretches at a time, but my body woke up like clockwork at 2:00 a.m., buzzing with anxiety.

"Sleep when the baby sleeps," people said. What a joke. My anxiety was through the roof, causing insomnia for weeks on end. I would stay awake all night and then care for him all day, trying to rest during his catnaps and crying on and off uncontrollably. I walked around the neighborhood in circles, feeling disconnected from the strangers' loving stares at my adorable baby.

I thought about the Twelve Steps, how helpful they would be at a time like this, but it was as though they were just out of my reach. I could recite them in my sleep, my intellect knowing them by heart, but emotionally I couldn't access them. My perfectionism kicked in hard. Nothing my husband did was right, and everything I did was wrong. I desperately needed help but didn't want to assign it to anyone for fear of them messing it all up. I had always wanted to be a mother, dammit, and I was going to figure this out. It's just a baby. Sleep, eat, poop, repeat. How hard could it be?

I rocked and shushed and bounced and swayed until my eyes rolled back in my head. He still only napped for twenty minutes at a time. I read every parenting book about catnappers and postpartum anxiety and googled "how to relax into motherhood," vowing to figure it all out. At 2:00 a.m. I would wake up again, wide eyed and scared of the dark.

The only other time in my life that I was unable to sleep was after a long night of cocaine. I'd quietly sneak back into my New York City walk-up, inhaling weed and swallowing the Xanax my father gave me to come down from the high. Scurrying into bed, I'd lie beside Ryan and grab his hand, synchronizing my pulse with his to assure me I wasn't going to die. Eight years later I was back in the dark again with full-blown depression and insomnia, only this time from something I had begged for—motherhood. After the marital crisis, the reckoning, the repair—my perfect baby was in the next room sleeping soundly. And here I was on the living room couch riddled with fear, headlamp around my face, reading spiritual literature until the sun came up. A constant reminder of my darkest days.

By week six, it became very clear that something was wrong. Despite how much therapy or time in the program I had, it was as though a thick fog followed me wherever I went. The anxiety and sadness were unmanageable, and I was unable to show up for myself, my husband, and my baby the way I wanted to. I had reverted back to my hardwiring for perfection as though I had never learned any other coping skill in my entire life.

I tried to control everything about motherhood—sleep schedules, mealtimes, and bedtime routines—all while being unable to emotionally regulate. I cried when I changed him, bounced him incessantly, and fed him any combination of breast milk and formula I could so that he would sleep for longer stretches. I panicked when my body woke me up in the middle of the night, wondering how the hell I was going to take care of this baby on no sleep.

Thankfully, I had enough time living in solution-based thinking that I called a sober friend and told her how much I was struggling. When she referred me to Step Ten and I took my inventory, I realized that I was living with some painful character defects—control being the most dominant. I wanted my labor, delivery, and postpartum experience to look a certain way and it didn't, and I simply couldn't handle it. Even in recognizing my own powerlessness, I still couldn't find my way into the solution on my own.

I had to reckon with my labor and delivery not going at all according to plan, breastfeeding not being something I loved, sleep schedules not coming easily. I had to let the entire vision I had of myself as a new mom collapse, love myself through all the ugly bits, and redefine what motherhood meant to me.

My friend recommended a psychiatrist who had experience with sober folks, assuring me he wouldn't put me on medication that was highly addictive. I called and got in as soon as I could. I began taking medicine for both my depression and my insomnia that day. Within a week, I was light-years better. I could function without hysterically crying, and though I still had insomnia for some time, I could remind myself, *this too shall pass*.

I was able to access the Steps again, thanks to medication, and I now had an experience in recovery that showed me the dire necessity for outside help, depending on the circumstance. Not only was I humbled by motherhood, and apologetic toward every mother I'd ever judged who came before me, but I was rocketed into a level of compassion for people everywhere who are in therapy and recovery and still need medication.

I also started psychotherapy with a wonderful woman who taught me about compassion in a way I hadn't yet practiced. Layer one of a self-compassion practice happened when I finally removed the guilt and shame of my past behavior and started forgiving myself for who I was and what I did as an addict. Layer two, however, went a step further, calling me to the table to love and honor myself as a new mom who was truly doing the best she could at the time.

As I stabilized, I relied heavily on the Steps to help me through. When I snapped at Ryan, I was able to apologize and ask for what I needed. When I tried to control Jack's ever-changing sleep schedule, I learned to surrender more deeply. When the night rolled in, I still dreaded the pending insomnia. Instead of fighting it, though, I immersed myself in bouts of spiritual literature on the couch, reminding myself that this moment in my life was only temporary.

One of the greatest gifts of this dark time was watching my judgment shatter, another handful of core beliefs unraveling in the face of this new experience that begged me to show up differently. *Easy does it* became my motto as I fumbled through that first year, using the Steps, counseling, and medicine to not only comfort me but also bring me back to life.

Eventually, I was ready to try for a second child. I was sure that the proof of making a perfect baby three years before would let the controller inside of me off the hook, allowing me to just enjoy the process of trying to get pregnant. Nope. As soon as we decided to try, I was right back where I started, much like people describe after a long stretch sober and then a relapse. I was controlling every aspect of my cycle and when and where my husband and I would fuck.

Once again, I got pregnant rather quickly, elated at my body's ability to make a human. And then, like clockwork, days into the positive pregnancy test, there was blood on the toilet paper. The sinking in my gut. The terror of another loss. I rushed to any doctor I could see, as my ob-gyn was unavailable on such short notice. I wept as a random stranger swirled a wand inside me, looking for a sac.

"Oh yes, you're definitely having a spontaneous abortion," she said dispassionately.

"A what? I'm sorry, is that the same thing as a miscarriage?"

She was as sterile and clinical as her dark gray office, the lack of expression on her face as cold as the temperature of my naked body under the paper gown. She left the room and I sobbed, rushing to the bathroom to roll toilet paper around my underwear to contain the blood. *Not again. Not now. Not like this.* I called Ryan and again, he tried to be compassionate but remained very removed, thankful that the loss was so early, when the baby was nothing but a cluster of cells.

If I thought I was afraid the first time, I hadn't seen anything yet. In the months to follow, I tracked my ovulation like a hawk tracks its prey, hunting down my husband and trying to act horny when all I really wanted was his goddamn sperm. Each month I bought the earliest pregnancy-detection tests, only to find out that I was indeed not pregnant.

By month six, I wondered what was wrong with me. I tried to get in to see a fertility doctor, and when I did, she found some scarring on my uterus that she thought might be to blame. It also could have been the remnants from my C-section, or just a random artifact from the imaging. She suggested I try acupuncture and come back in six more months if I wasn't pregnant.

Being a health-care practitioner, I was willing to try anything, though I was skeptical about the connection between needles on the surface of my skin and making babies. What did one have to do with another? I expressed my concerns to the doctor, and she assured me that acupuncture can do wonders for fertility.

The acupuncturist's name was Maria; she was a beautiful

woman with a soft-spoken voice. For several sessions, I let her stick needles all the way from the top of my head to the base of my feet, meditating when I was left alone in the room because I didn't know what else to do. A vision came to mind during these sessions, one where I was on my back in the middle of a wide-open grassy field, holding my baby in the air as the sun shined down. It was a glorious image, and I tried to let the feelings this image conjured up course through my veins. Then, after forty-five minutes or so, Maria came in and removed the needles. I went back out into the world, watching the cars and the mothers and the babies go by, painfully aware that I was not pregnant.

The next month, I was at my office in Santa Monica and knew I was ovulating. I had an insane urge to have my husband come by and fuck me right then and there.

"Ryan, I need you to come to the office right now. Don't ask any questions," I said.

"Everything okay?" he asked, concerned.

"Oh yes," I whispered, lowering my voice a few octaves to conjure up my best phone sex operator impression.

To my inner controller's delight, we fucked right there on the treatment table in between clients. I've never asked him what he thought about that moment, but God bless his little heart for jumping on the crazy train and going for a ride. When I could finally take a pregnancy test, every stick came back negative. I held the tests up to the light and searched for the faintest pink lines, driving myself crazy, thinking I saw them when they most certainly weren't there. Fortunately, I had an acupuncture appointment that same day, and I sat with Maria, disgruntled and disheartened.

"How are you?" she asked lovingly.

"Not pregnant *again*. I'm so fucking tired."

She tilted her head to the side compassionately.

"Let's put some extra needles into your temples today to soothe your nervous system."

I nodded, darting my eyes as the tears began to fall. She handed me a box of tissues and I wiped the snot from the edge of my nose and lay back. She left the room and there I was again, alone with my thoughts. I noticed the familiar buzzing, random ideas racing back and forth, and I breathed slowly and deeply until they settled. Finally, the manager inside of me was tired, and she slipped out of her seat as CEO for the moment.

That's when I felt the sink—the absolute place of rest my nervous system had so much trouble accessing over the past few months. From somewhere deep in my belly, a strange image appeared in my mind of a tadpole splashing around in water. *That's odd*, I thought. I had never before (or since) imagined that, and I wondered what it meant. It went away as quickly as it came, and the session ended, leaving me slightly more hopeful and a lot calmer.

When I got home, I continued to test for several more days, holding the stupid stick up to the light and straining my eyes to find the pink line. Nothing. But still, my period was late. I finally had the notion to buy a test that said either "pregnant" or "not pregnant," instead of decoding watery lines. One day in April, seven months into my second pregnancy journey, I got the word I had been longing for. I was pregnant. Exhilarated and terrified, I had a trip planned to New York the following week with my best friend, and I couldn't think of a better way to celebrate.

During our stay, we walked the streets, shopped at the stores, and ate all the delicious foods. I put on a fancy dress one night when we were headed to an event and noticed a red-tinged stain on my underwear. *No. No, no, no. Not again.* I wiped myself several more times. There was no more blood, leaving me confused. I told my girlfriend, and we resolved to take what was happening one moment at a time.

I got through the evening with bouts of joy and terror, forgetting about my body's misgivings and then rushing to the bathroom to check if the bleeding had returned. For the next few days, the toilet paper stained a reddish brown on and off. I was frantic, but aside from admitting myself to an emergency room, there were no facilities I could get into before my flight home. Calling ahead, I found a place I could go the second the plane landed back in LA, and I attempted to enjoy the rest of my trip while I could, repeating the mantra "Be where your feet are."

Ryan picked me up at the airport with Jack in the car seat. He was smiling and supportive as he drove me to the women's clinic. Mr. Hopeful. Mr. Casual. Mr. Trying-His-Best-but-Has-No-Fucking-Clue.

I checked in and stood at the counter. To the receptionist, I was just another patient who had to fill out paperwork. But for me, this moment of reckoning would be the moment I was either a growing mother or a grieving mother. The nurse practitioner walked me to the back and welcomed me. She nodded compassionately as she listened to my concerns.

"Well, let's get you in this gown and do an ultrasound. It's quite early, but we should be able to get some good information. I'll be back in a few minutes."

I undressed, grateful to at least be at the point where I could know something. The not knowing, as usual, had left me exhausted and afraid, despite my efforts to trust the process. In this entire pregnancy journey, I had relied only a little on prayer and meditation, still falling back on my old patterns of control, management, and manipulation.

To my delight, we saw the sac, and there in that random clinic in El Segundo I saw my baby for the first time. The bleeding, said the nurse, was likely just implantation bleeding, remnants of the egg burrowing into my uterus to find her home for the next nine months. She handed me a picture of the ultrasound.

As I looked closely, I realized that the baby was as small as a tadpole. *Holy shit*, I thought. The acupuncturist. The image. What if that was my intuition telling me there was a baby inside me, swimming around and seeking refuge? That my body was divinely intelligent and knew exactly what to do, especially when my mind didn't. I rushed outside and held the picture up to the driver's-side window. Ryan smirked with a "See! I told you not to worry!" look on his face.

That day was such a happy day. I spent the first trimester sicker than ever, gagging and puking at the sight and smell of everything, but I hung on to my gratitude like a child hangs on to their mother the first day of school. I felt so lucky that this baby was growing inside of me, my sickness a constant reminder of her presence.

Early in the second trimester, I hit a smooth patch, feeling a lot less nauseous and a lot more energized. I had a growing belly and a buoyant heart, taking trips with friends on the weekends and living my best before-baby-comes life. In the shower on a girls' trip to Ojai, I noticed a rash on my belly, exacerbated by the hot water. *That's odd*, I thought. I googled it and saw posts about rashes on women whose skin stretched like Silly Putty. I felt at ease. A rash seemed so simple compared to a miscarriage. Bring it on. At my next gynecologist appointment, I mentioned it to my doctor. She stopped.

"Is it itchy?" she asked.

"Not at all," I said.

Her silence scared me.

"What?" I asked, knowing she was stirring over something.

"Let's just do a blood test. I want to check something."

I stared, my eyes reminding her that if she didn't disclose what she was thinking I would get on the internet immediately and find out for myself.

"I don't want you to start looking this up and getting freaked out," she warned. "I just want to check your liver enzymes. You don't have most of the signs or symptoms, but I just want to do my due diligence and be sure."

I went cold. As I continued to stare, I felt my anxiety rise.

"What are you testing for?"

She sighed. "It's called cholestasis—it's just one of those pregnancy things that can happen where the liver functions more slowly than normal. Let's talk more about it if it becomes an issue."

I tried to memorize the word *cholestasis*, saying it again and again so I wouldn't google it incorrectly. As it turns out, I did not match the clinical presentation whatsoever; this condition mostly affected Pacific Asian women in the third trimester and was characterized by no rash and insane itchiness in the hands and feet. *Whew*, I thought. I let her take my blood and went on my merry way, leaving the anxiety in my doctor's lap, since she was being paranoid over nothing. She was just the hypervigilant type of doctor, crossing every *t* and dotting every *i*.

A few days later she texted with good news. My liver enzymes were normal. Another huge sigh of relief. That weekend was blissful. Our growing family spent time outside, playing hide-and-seek and basking in the sun. On Tuesday the next week, I came out of yoga and saw six missed calls and a voicemail from my doctor's office: "Please call Dr. Alamen back. It's urgent."

Fuck. I pulled over and called back.

"Hi, Samantha. So, I know your liver enzymes were normal, but we were still waiting on the results of the bile acid test, which is the gold standard for diagnosing cholestasis. Unfortunately, it came back very high. You need to start medication to lower the levels right away and make an appointment with a high-risk doctor, which you have to do anyway because of your age," she told me.

As I listened to her talk, I had an out-of-body experience. My clinical brain was dissecting everything she said and waiting to hang up so I could research the shit out of this diagnosis, but my emotional body was swirling and stressing and pushing up against this news to make it not true.

"What does this mean? What can happen to me and the baby? Does medication cure it?" I asked.

"Well, moms have to be monitored constantly to make sure the bile acid levels don't go too high."

I paused. "Because then what?" I asked urgently.

She waited for a beat.

"With this diagnosis, the rate of stillbirth increases. It's still very low, about 2 percent, but with careful monitoring of mom and baby and an early delivery, it is usually fine."

"Wait, what? Stillbirth? Are you saying that I can have a dead baby inside of me that I would have to deliver?" I was six months pregnant and finding out I had a condition that could kill my child. *This could not be happening.*

Despite my doctor urging me to stay off the internet, I went straight into Google land, reading harrowing tales of mothers who had heard their baby's heartbeats at an appointment on a Monday, and then delivered their dead baby on a Tuesday. I scheduled the first appointment that I could with the "best" high-risk doctor in LA. After a two-hour wait, I sat in the treatment room as the doctor carefully reviewed my chart.

"Your condition isn't bad," he said stoically. "Your numbers are not too high, and you don't really match the other women who come in here with it. They are usually itching to the point of insanity. So that's good."

I tried to stay calm as I asked the hardest questions.

"So why does this happen? How can I prevent it from worsening? This is so scary—I just want to do everything I can."

He spun around in his chair.

"You know, we don't really know why the babies die. Mom comes in for her appointment and we check the vitals, and then the baby dies overnight. We just don't know why."

I listened, horrified. He continued.

"We check the baby's heartbeat and it's perfect, mom goes to sleep, and she wakes up in the morning to a dead baby."

Stunned in silence.

He kept going. "It has something to do with the bile acids being toxic for the baby, but why it happens in the third trimester and why it happens so suddenly, we still don't know. The babies are here, and then they're dead." He finished and spun back around, typing notes into the computer.

I tried to reconcile with his lack of affect at the phrase "dead baby" while wrapping my head around how I was going to survive the rest of this pregnancy with those words careening in my nervous system.

That night, when I woke up to pee, I got back in bed and put my hand on my belly. No movement. I immediately panicked, lying in the dark and gently nudging the baby side to side to wait for any sign of life. Nothing. I turned to one side and then to the other. After forty-five minutes of agony—hiccups. *Jesus Christ*, I thought. I relished every jump of my belly, every palpable sign of life, and as I drifted back to sleep, I wondered if she'd still be there in the morning.

What that doctor seemed to carelessly forget was that I was entering the third and scariest trimester for women with this condition, and the fact that insomnia is also a common pregnancy symptom around this time. These facts, combined with the memory of the words "dead baby," circled around in my mind on every sleepless night. I often stared at the popcorn ceiling, wondering if this would in fact be the night that I lost my baby. In one of these quiet moments, it occurred to me that I needed to reroute the recovery catchphrase "one day at a time" so it was applicable now.

Months seven and eight were a turning point. I could either fall into a pit of anxiety and despair, obsessively reading every possible outcome of this diagnosis, or I could try and radically surrender *again*. I had already spent hours ruminating over the worst-case scenario, thrusting myself awake when my body desperately needed sleep. I had hit the wall and was once again granted the gift of desperation. I could feel myself wanting to control my pregnancy, and so instead I imagined a positive outcome, the vision of my beautiful baby in my arms.

I made space for rest and the whisper of God. My sober experience had taught me so much: If I kept a death-grip on this situation, I would send my nervous system into a constant state of fight-or-flight and place more stress on my body and my baby. I needed something to say and feel that brought me tactile comfort. So I took the language in recovery and made it very specific: *One kick at a time, my baby is okay. One kick at a time, I can trust that she is still alive, and I can let myself sleep. One kick at a time, my baby and I will get through this scary pregnancy.*

I let divine words wash over me. *Your perfect baby is coming*, she'd say quietly. Every time I slid back into fear and control, I put my hand on my belly and stroked my baby. We were in this together, and perhaps the idea of mothering would begin much earlier than expected—a chance to teach my child what courage feels like, flooding my system with the power of surrender to calm the chaos.

At one of my last high-risk appointments, I lay back on the table expecting the usual—absolutely no warmth or empathy from the doctor albeit a thorough report on the baby's size, development, and vital signs. Staring at the ceiling, I recited the serenity prayer silently. *God, grant me the serenity to accept the things I cannot change (this doctor's personality, the results of this checkup, the fear I still have about this baby dying), the courage to change the things I can (my mindset, my practice of prayer and meditation, my ability to ask for support), and the wisdom to know the difference.*

After thirty minutes, he had me sit up, a familiar spot where I stared at the back of his head and my legs rustled against the paper covering the table, soon to be thrown away and refreshed for the next expectant mother. I decided to speak up.

"You know, Doc, I want to tell you something. When you talked to me about cholestasis the last time, you mentioned the phrase 'dead babies' on repeat. I'm not saying you should avoid telling women the truth about their diagnoses, but I think you ought to be more discerning with your words. All the women in this clinic are high risk and know their baby could die. What they need from you is a mix of knowledge and compassion. They can go to the internet for the rest if they choose," I said.

He listened.

"I'm going to think about that," he said.

He turned back to his computer, the final moment before the session was about to wrap up. Then he said hurriedly, "Lie back down."

Weird, I thought. My phone started buzzing and it was Ryan, wondering where I was. I texted and told him I was supposed to be finishing up my appointment but that the doctor asked me to lie down, so I didn't know what was happening. He replied, "Don't worry, I'm nearby." This was also odd, since he rarely followed up on my appointment days.

"I don't like the blood flow to the umbilical artery," the doctor said.

I had no idea what he meant, other than it wasn't good. This was the guy who could talk about dead babies over coffee and French toast without breaking a sweat, and now he was expressing concern. My anxiety gauge shot to level ten. I texted Ryan, who drove to where I was and waited in the lobby.

"You can sit back up," the doctor said.

Once again, I rolled my shirt down and sat up, this time a lot less relaxed.

"I checked to make sure the blood flow was normal to the baby's brain, and it is. When is your C-section?"

"It's not until Sunday. Why? Should I move it up?"

He pondered this question with a tilt of his head.

"Well, you could go home tonight and go to the hospital tomorrow . . . or you could go right now. Either way."

I sat there in disbelief.

"So, the same doctor who told me babies can die overnight with no explanation is suggesting I go home for a night and then go to the hospital in the morning? No thanks, Doc, I think I'll head right over."

When I saw Ryan in the lobby, I told him to drop me at the hospital and drive home to pack my bag. I gave him a giant squeeze and as we let go, we looked at each other, eyes wide with terror and excitement.

"I guess we're having this baby!"

My gynecologist called me with the new plan. I would stay in the hospital for monitoring for two nights and have the C-section on a Sunday morning to get the baby as close to thirty-eight weeks as possible. That way, the lungs could be fully developed. If anything happened beforehand, I'd be right where I needed to be.

The next two evenings proved very difficult. I barely slept, between anxiety, beeping monitors, and practitioners constantly repositioning the heart-rate monitor to a new spot on my belly to make sure the baby was safe. Finally, the day had come. I woke up on Sunday, December 9, at 7:00 a.m. to the nurses adjusting the IV drip.

"Are you ready to meet your baby?"

I sat up, nodded, and asked for a minute alone with Ryan as we put our gowns on. I dropped my head in my hands and sobbed, a thick and heavy cry leaving my body. I was exhausted, overwhelmed, and utterly relieved that I had made it to this day— that my baby had made it to this day. Unless something happened between that moment and when they pulled her out of me, we were both still there, alive and kicking.

I walked into the operating room and looked around. As I watched the health-care professionals go through their checklists, I couldn't help but think of women as nothing less than superheroes, exquisitely brave, walking through hell and high water on this journey called motherhood. As much as I hated the high-risk doctor's bedside manner, I trusted his expertise unequivocally. Both he and my gynecologist were in the room and ready to go.

As I flattened out on the table, the familiar rustling of the medical sheets now a comfort, I felt my anxiety rise. I took long, deep breaths and heard my playlist fade into the background. Within a few minutes I entered a deep state of relaxation.

The surgery began as the scalpel brushed the skin above my pubic bone. They were quiet when they needed to be and then cracked jokes as they rearranged my insides to reach my uterus.

"Well, I didn't expect this playlist!" said the high-risk doctor, popping his head over the curtain separating us. It was a mix of pop hits and hip-hop—a surefire way to keep me in a mental dance while I was going through physical hell.

"We're almost there," said my gynecologist. "I just want to remind you that we might not hear the baby cry. Try not to be alarmed. The lungs are the last to develop, and she's coming out early."

I was warned that I would feel some pressure, just like the first time. I felt myself rise off the table, relieved that they were finally taking this baby out of my toxic body. And as "God Is a Woman" played, I heard the best sound of my life. My strong, fierce baby girl came out screaming, demanding that I know she wasn't just okay—she was goddamn perfect. As I listened to her cry, the high pitch echoing through the operating room, I felt the holy presence of God. Ryan held her and quivered through his words.

"My baby girl. My sweet baby girl."

In the weeks that followed, I entered a deep state of gratitude. Every midnight feeding, every growth spurt, every wince of pain from the surgery were blips on the radar in comparison to having Charly in my arms. I was completely and utterly in love and awe of this baby who could have died and instead brought me back to life. Who I held and kissed and coddled every chance I could because I was the lucky mom whose story had a happy ending. Who I cherished and played with and learned from because I was so ready to be a mother again.

Charly proved that the mother I had imagined myself to be was in fact there, she just had a very rough first go. She taught me that kids have a divine intelligence, a knowing of what they need, if only parents can surrender long enough to notice it. She showed me what life was all about—love and trust and joy and growth—the kinds of things people understand when they've brushed the back of death's head.

The journey into motherhood was riddled with loss, fear, and a frantic attempt to regain control. This part of my life, like every part that is new to me in recovery, knocked me on my ass and had me grasping at an old way of thinking, behaving, and coping. I spent some time in old neurological patterns—I worried, I googled, I obsessed. But I also quickly remembered I had other choices. I knew that praying to God to spare my baby didn't feel right, because that inherently implies that I subscribe to a God that picks and chooses who gets to live or die.

Since I certainly didn't believe in a God that would kill babies, my concept of God had to expand yet again. I had the hard facts. My baby could live, or she could die—so now what? What did prayer and meditation look like under these terrible circumstances? It looked like meditating on the vision of a healthy baby in my arms. It looked like taking the utmost care of my body, so the baby had a beautiful place to rest. It looked like asking God to help me trust this pregnancy one kick at a time and to stay in the day so I could be present for my life.

When you reach Step Ten, you enter the present moment. You're not (as) haunted by the ghosts of the past. That doesn't mean you aren't human and that you won't make mistakes. What it does mean, though, is that you can point yourself in a solution-oriented direction when a new problem arises. You can take inventory of your behaviors and apologize. You can start your day again at any time, spiritually speaking. Through these new practices, you have a sense of self-worth that isn't contingent on outside things. It's earned, the emotional scars proof that you've survived every one of your worst days. My hope is that it's not something you're willing to give up.

AN ALTERNATE LOOK AT STEP TEN

Ryan and I buy a tiny fixer-upper four miles from the ocean because that's all we can afford. For the next few years, we fix up one room at a time, hoping the market turns such that we can sell, take our equity, and buy up.

During this time, Ryan's business starts to take off, and we have stronger income to support a larger home. The market also becomes primed for sellers—a perfect opportunity to duck and run. I call Arianna, a friend who is like a sister, throughout the entire process.

"What if it doesn't sell?" she says. "Inventory is very low right now, so it might be hard to find another home."

I let her give me unsolicited advice and choose not to respond, moving forward with my plans. After many weeks, we put the house on the market and buyers are everywhere, coming in well over asking and guaranteeing the sale of the house. Oddly, having no desire to move, Arianna starts sending me links to a few houses she might buy, and I write back with a simple thumbs-up emoji. I start to wonder if she is struggling with my move, and I call to talk.

"I don't know if I'm misinterpreting this, but it feels like there's some jealousy going on with you. Is that true?"

She pauses for a moment.

"Of course I'm jealous," she says blankly.

I am shocked and hurt.

"Thank you for telling me that. That's really hard to hear, considering all that I have been through, so I'm going to take a little space." I do, and when we talk again, she sobs, admitting that she is struggling with her marriage and asking if I can carry the emotional load of the friendship for now. I tell her I will try my best.

Weeks go by and I don't hear from her. I try calling to tell her I'm in escrow and she texts back a simple "Congrats." I call several times until she picks up, and when she does, I let her have it.

"I don't understand why you can't be happy for me. You're not supposed to do this! You're my chosen family. Are you only able to be supportive when my life sucks?"

"I don't want to do this with you," she says after a moment of silence. She hangs up.

At this point, we've made it all the way to maintenance mode in Step Ten. What might it look like to forget to apply it in this situation? And what might it look like to remember what I've worked so hard for?

Reaction 1: It's Not Me; It's You

I think about the conversation and feel justified in my reaction. Even though I know Arianna is struggling in her marriage, I think she should be able to get past it and be happy for me. She has seen me recover from an extramarital affair, miscarriages, and serious family dysfunction. Don't I deserve to have something good in my life? If she can't move her own shit to the side and celebrate me, then that's on her.

I call her less and less. Even though I miss her terribly, I think she owes me an apology. Essentially, I want her to show up differently in the friendship because her current behavior makes me feel unloved, unseen, and uncared for. It makes me feel out of control. I want the old Arianna back so I don't have to grieve the loss of any more female figures in my life. As I cling to my anger, the distance between us grows, and I am heartbroken.

Reaction 2: Remembering That Growth Is an Inside Job

I feel the anger and betrayal and it is real—I want friends who bask in my success and stand beside me when my light shines brightly. I want friends who don't get jealous of me like my sister did my entire life. I want proof that I can have and keep healthy friendships after all the hell I've lived through.

I realize that several wounds had been triggered, and from that space I lashed out. I didn't let her have her own experience. I tried to force her to be happy for me so I could have the friendship I wanted. After taking a quick inventory, I call her again.

"I want to apologize for my anger and for not holding space for your feelings. I'm sorry this is hard for you, and I want to know how I can support you."

There is a long silence, followed by the choking back of tears.

"I'm struggling so much right now, Sam. I know I've always been so supportive, but right now I need you to show up for me. Can you do that?"

I ask how I can support her and tell her I love her. We hang up, both feeling closer to each other after the conversation.

Wrap-Up: The Beauty of Maintenance Mode

Communication is tricky when emotions run high. Old habits come back, and defense mechanisms show up when we're tired, triggered, and afraid. Sometimes it feels good to stay mad. Once that adrenaline wears off, though, the aftermath of reactive behavior is what is known in recovery as an emotional hangover.

The longer I stay sober, the less tolerance I have for these hangovers. They physically exhaust me and mentally beat me up, and because I have deep reverence for my well-being, I can't live in that space for long. What I do, then, is take inventory of what happened, sometimes alone, sometimes with the help of a therapist or sponsor, and sometimes in the quiet presence of God, and dig at what the underlying cause of the behavior is. I can find compassion for myself and imagine what I would have liked to say or do instead.

Then, I can honestly approach the person I had the interaction with and explain myself, making quick amends for my words or actions with a promise to work on myself moving forward. Why does this matter? Well, my head can hit the pillow each night free and clear of guilt or shame. Luckily, I love myself way too much to choose self-sabotage over my peace of mind, but it isn't easy.

Even at fifteen years sober, I make mistakes constantly, for which I can thankfully take a quick inventory and apologize when it's called for. This does a few things.

1. It clears my conscience so that I don't give my internal critic ammunition to speak more loudly.

2. It connects me with the people I have hurt by showing them my humanity, and often the outcome results in more closeness; there is now proof that I can do a hard thing, survive it, and still be loved and accepted.

3. It holds me accountable for my behavior by understanding where it came from, owning it, and making a commitment to do better next time.

In Step Ten, we have a universal way of cleaning up our side of the street, so to speak—a way to review the day and see where we did well and where we could have done better. Step Ten provides a framework for how to rectify our wrongs without carrying around anger, guilt, and shame. That's not just powerful; it's life-changing. So where do we make our start?

STEP TEN: YOUR VERSION

When you start making a daily practice of taking your own inventory, it's rather quick and simple. Following is a step-by-step process that you can use every day. As a reminder, in Step Ten, we've "continued to take personal inventory and when we were wrong promptly admitted it."[20]

1. Take a few minutes toward the end of your day to do a mental review. Maybe it's in the shower, or maybe it's in the few minutes before bed. Try not to make it another "thing to do," and instead work it into something you already do.

2. Go over whom you spoke to (including yourself), how you spoke to them, and what you did well or could have done better.

3. If there is something you wish you'd handled better, consider what happened and how, moving forward, you can behave differently.

4. If there are amends to make, write them down in your journal and pause. After a solid night's sleep, when the nervous system is rested and restored, you can make things right.

As mentioned earlier, there is a saying in recovery that I love: "Resentment is like drinking poison and waiting for the other person to die." Sometimes anger feels so damn good. It's almost a high in and of itself. And we can stay angry—that is our choice. But when the seduction fades, the only person who suffers is us. If the goal is peace, joy, and freedom—a life worth living—then no matter what happens, we must get honest, take responsibility, and change accordingly.

---

20 Alcoholics Anonymous World Services, *Twelve Steps and Twelve Traditions*, 88.

11

MAGIC TRICKS

STEP ELEVEN, AS WRITTEN IN the Big Book of Alcoholics Anonymous, goes like this:

> [We] sought through prayer and meditation to improve our conscious contact with God as we understood Him, praying only for knowledge of His will for us and the power to carry that out.[21]

The language of this step may still sound religious and antiquated, but we have done some significant work to reimagine the Steps so that they resonate with us. We have also established a power source that we believe in, allowing us to trust the unknown in a brand-new way. Step Eleven arrives at just the right time, introducing the practice of meditation into the fabric of our lives. This practice has become the conduit to my highest self, the channel to an inner guidance system that had been covered up by a lifetime of drinking, drugs, people-pleasing, and shame. To this day,

---

21 Alcoholics Anonymous World Services, *Twelve Steps and Twelve Traditions* (New York: Alcoholics Anonymous World Services, 1981), 96.

it continues to be the gateway to my intuition, the clearest path to accessing power beyond my cerebral capabilities.

When I first lie down to meditate, I notice a pulsating energy at the surface of my skin; my mind is racing, and my body is clenching. This is the place where, if I attach to my thoughts, I can become highly reactive. This is the place where I can give energy to a narrative that tells me I am not worthy of love or connection. It takes several minutes to calm down, my intellect tossing ideas back and forth until I become the witness, not the victim, of them. Eventually, at around the ten-minute mark, I sink. This is the moment when my mind takes a back seat to my body as I settle into the earth, where I feel calm and held. When I operate from this place, it's as if my thoughts and ideas rise from the belly up, their truth centered in my gut rather than my mind. They always feel clear and compassionate. When I gain access to this place, I am in conscious contact with my higher power—with the truest and most beautiful version of my *self*.

PATTERNS DON'T DISAPPEAR; THEY TAKE NEW SHAPE

Years into my sobriety and after several Step Fours, I continued to have a chip on my shoulder when I would see my father. No matter how well intentioned I was, how mindful I tried to be, I was short tempered and reactive in his presence. All would be going well and then he would say or do something that felt violating to the grown sober woman I had become.

"Did Mom call you recently?" he would ask. "Did she say anything about me?"

No matter how many times I asked him not to put me in the middle of their dysfunctional mess, he always did.

"Are you still giving Jessica pills?" I'd respond back, with my head cocked to the side. His eyes would dodge mine and the enablement disgusted me. If he were truly sorry, he would stop. "Are you fucking serious, Dad?"

The codependency he and my sister had on one another made my blood boil. No matter how many times I had worked the Steps around this issue, I couldn't seem to let my father off the hook for putting me in the middle of his mess or keeping my family members sick. I couldn't hold on to the notion of him as a sick man. I couldn't forgive him for violating my sense of safety. "Stop feeding Jessica's addiction!" I'd shout. I always put the control in his hands—clueless about how to set and hold a real boundary—which, of course, gave my power away.

My father was a three-time cancer survivor and had more than ten years free and clear of malignant melanoma. On a routine checkup, though, the doctors noticed a plunge in his platelet count that alarmed them. Upon further testing, they diagnosed him with a rare autoimmune disorder called immune thrombocytopenia, or ITP for short, which is a condition where your own body attacks its platelets, leaving you at risk of bleeding out. His doctors said it was not a life-threatening condition, and that medical management worked well.

I had just given birth to Charly when he got his first steroid shot. That boosted his platelet count quite a bit and he was able to visit me in LA and meet her. Shortly after the trip, his platelet count dropped again, and the doctors tried a few more things before considering surgery to remove his spleen. He was seventy-five years old and overweight, so they decided to try a strong drug before surgery because it was less risky. I spoke with him over FaceTime on a Wednesday in April 2019. He looked ragged.

"What's wrong, Dad?" I asked softly. "You don't look well."

"I'm not sure, but I keep getting really out of breath when I walk the dog. It started ever since I went on the new medication. Your sister thinks I should go to the ER, but I think she's exaggerating."

As you know by now, my father had a history of denial, so I chimed in carefully and strategically so he could hear me.

"Dad, I think she might be right. If you're not comfortable with that, can you at least call your doctor who prescribed the new medication and tell him about your symptoms?"

Fortunately, he was open to that and quickly made an appointment with his general physician and the oncologist. Both doctors cleared him of anything serious and told him not to worry. Two days later I went out for a walk with Ryan, Jack, and baby Charly. My phone was on silent so I could plug out of the external world and into nature. When I returned home, there were several text messages from my sister urging me to call her, telling me that Dad was unconscious and being rushed to the hospital. I collapsed on the sidewalk and called her right back. She was hysterical.

"Sam, oh my God," she said between sobs, "I swear it's this *fucking* medication! I *knew* he should've gone to the ER! What if he's not okay? Oh my God, this can't be happening!"

I tried to calm her down and find out what happened. She shared that he had been found unconscious in his elevator with his dog Billy circling his limp body. A neighbor discovered him and called 911. He was rushed to a local hospital, where they called my sister and informed her of his status—alive but in critical condition.

I tried to compose myself. My sister gave me the number for the hospital. After we hung up, I called to get more information. The ER doctor didn't say much except that they were monitoring him and would call me with updates. Meanwhile, my sister was driving to the hospital in a state of panic. Within twenty minutes, I received a call back from the doctor.

"Samantha?"

I could tell by his voice that it wasn't good.

"No, please, God, no," I whispered.

"I didn't want to call your sister because she's driving. I'm so sorry. Your father died."

A sound emerged from my body that only those who have experienced a death can know. A primal wail unlike any other cry, the kind that comes from a cellular place when a part of who you are dies. In that moment, I lost something I could never get back—a chance to reckon fully with my anger, a moment to heal the deep wounds between us, a world in which both my parents were still alive. No matter how much my father triggered me, I had no idea until that moment how much I counted on him always being there.

No one ever found out for sure what he died from. My sister refused an autopsy because she couldn't imagine his body being cut open, though I so badly wanted to know what happened. Without answers, my sister and I had to organize his cremation, spread his ashes, and plan a celebration-of-life party.

I took a flight the next day and stayed with Jessica in her modern apartment in northern New Jersey. I realized quickly that she was not the slightest bit sober. Steeping in her own denial, she lashed out every time I asked her what was wrong.

"You seem to be having trouble focusing," I said. "We have so much to plan, and I need your help. What's going on with you?"

"*Nothing!*" she shouted.

At one point the arguing escalated so badly that I packed my bags, threatening to stay at a nearby hotel because the insanity of a dead father and an addicted sister was too much to bear. When she realized I was about to leave, she apologized, and we cried together in our disbelief and devastation that Dad was gone. On top of that, our mother was acutely manic, heightening the grief of it all. As was often the case, we were financially and emotionally on our own.

The next few days are both vivid and hazy. I remember holding my father's cold face in the open casket, wanting so badly to feel it warm up again. I wondered if, like him, I could become a magician, doing and saying just the right thing to make him come back to life. His face seemed content, yet I knew he died well before his time, overwhelmed by financial fear and sick with emotional codependency. I remember inviting his dearest friends to the celebration-of-life party, the flowers I ordered, and the picture collages I made, but I have no idea what I said or how I functioned. What I remember most distinctly is what I was left with in the aftermath—a heart full of regret at the way I showed up in the last few years of his life.

The guilt and shame I felt about my own hostility sent me into a level of sickness that was new territory for me in all my years sober. It started with a declaration of how I would lose the baby weight and show the world how I bounced back after two kids. What seemed like a typical pursuit to get fit again quickly turned into a level of obsession and restriction over my food intake and body that I had never experienced before.

Every waking moment centered around what I would eat and how much I would move. I exercised for two to three hours and ate around 1,400 calories a day, carefully measuring each food group so I didn't go above my limit. I found great comfort in being able to control and manipulate my body in this way. It was the perfect distraction from my grief. Since I was powerless over my father's death, which left me riddled with pain, I tried to find power in any way that I could.

Defaulting to perfectionism, I lost the baby weight in no time and, in the process, received high praise. For a short while it felt like I had finally figured it out. *This* is how to get thin and shredded! *This* is how people win all the cash and prizes! *Finally*, I would be thin enough, pretty enough, and good enough. Finally, I could use this body to make some serious cash; people all over the world will want to buy what I am selling.

It is part of the human condition to seek access to power. It is also deeply ingrained in our cultural conditioning. The problem is that when we gain power from things outside of ourselves, it isn't real, and it doesn't last. Eventually, the house of cards collapses, and we are left with what they call in recovery a God-sized hole.

After nine months of running from the death of my father, I agreed to a date night with Ryan where we would each go into a flotation tank and then grab sushi. I felt panicked at the notion of being alone with my thoughts for sixty minutes straight and particularly terrified of how I would control my carbohydrate intake at dinner so I didn't gain weight.

We gave each other a kiss and went into our separate spheres. I undressed and got in the tank, taking a mental note of the irony as I closed the coffin-like top. I lay there in the silence with my eyes shut and observed my very busy mind. It raced back and forth with thoughts, most of which were about food, body, and exercise, and then at the forty-five-minute mark, it went quiet.

My intuitive voice appeared and asked, *Why are you punishing me?*

I was stunned by the question, but I had enough recovery to recognize that the voice was my highest self, my capital-S Self, and she had been shoved down into a dark compartment of my mind for these last nine months. When she finally appeared, she asked a hard and poignant question.

Am I punishing myself? I wondered. Suddenly, I saw my behavior as one giant escape mechanism from my shame. I had felt so guilty about the way I showed up in my relationship with my father before he passed that I couldn't forgive myself. I couldn't coexist in a body that was ashamed of its behavior, so instead I tried to make it disappear. I had so much self-loathing for the way I treated my dad that the only way I could handle my own behavior was to try and wipe out my own existence.

In the remaining fifteen minutes in the tank, I went into a meditation that linked my breath to a very important mantra. On every inhale I whispered, "I love you, Sam," and on every exhale I said, "I forgive you, Dad." I said it again and again until I felt it was time to switch. Deep breath in: "I love you, Dad." Deep breath out: "I forgive you, Sam." I wept in the tank as I said these words, knowing deep down that this was the work required to heal, and it had only just begun. That the only way to release my own guilt and shame was to forgive us both and douse us with love. That if I kept on running and sweating and starving, I would die too.

It was a long time before the attempt at controlling my body would let up, but I had made a start. I couldn't change what happened before, but I could continue to do the work now. I could also take this as a valuable lesson moving forward: Resentment, left untreated, can come back to haunt you in insidious ways.

AN ALTERNATE LOOK AT STEP ELEVEN

Deep into raising kids, Ryan stops going to Al-Anon. This pisses me off royally because it is not what he'd promised. After surviving a five-year extramarital affair, the only way I feel comfortable moving forward with him is if and only if he goes to therapy and works a Twelve Step program. Two kids later, all the work stops.

When we have arguments, my resentment is greater than the argument deserves because underneath I believe that we wouldn't have the argument at all had he been working a program. I lie in bed at night and pray to God that Ryan will work the Steps and just do what I want. Still nothing. I call my therapist and hash out my resentment.

"It sounds like your sense of self-worth is disrupted. You only believe you're justified in taking him back if he follows the protocol you've set out for him."

I think about it. "Yes, that's exactly right."

"I wonder if it's possible to imagine a happy marriage even if he never goes to another meeting or therapy again. Do you think you can trust that he would be faithful? That he loves you and is a wonderful husband and father regardless?"

Well, shit. I had never even considered that. I had a core belief that the only way a woman takes back a man who has committed this type of crime is if and only if he does a lifetime of work. Now, my therapist is challenging this belief and it's my job to consider it. I am furious.

This is a perfect opportunity to play out some responses.

Reaction 1: Hey, God, Can You Fix This Person?

My therapist's suggestion triggers me. I'm smart enough to know that I can reframe my perspective, but why should I? I want Ryan to do the work he never did so that a betrayal like his would never happen again. I spend weeks trying to convince him to go to meetings, therapy, or a healthy combination of both, and when I pray, I focus solely on receiving the outcome I long for.

"Dear God, whoever you are, please convince Ryan to work the Twelve Steps because if he doesn't, I don't think I can stay in the marriage. Amen." As you can imagine, my attempts are in vain. No amount of forcing, convincing, controlling, or manipulative prayer will get Ryan to do what I want. Faced with this reality, I have a choice to make. Will I stay and live in a perpetual state of anger, or will I go and leave this all behind?

Reaction 2: Hey, God, Can You Show Me What's Next?

I think about my therapist's words and know she has a point. The fact that Ryan isn't doing the work threatens my sense of self-worth. I am deeply attached to the idea that a woman like me does not take back a cheating partner unless he makes a lifelong commitment to change. Otherwise, how can I be sure he won't cheat again?

According to my therapist, my sense of security is directly contingent on my willingness to reframe my beliefs. Perhaps there is a world in which Ryan had broken my heart but would not break it again. Had cheated on me but was not a cheater. Had always loved me but made some big mistakes. Perhaps there is a world where Ryan made a commitment to change, even if he never went to another meeting or therapy session again.

The idea of strengthening this new belief infuriates me. Why do I always have to do the work? It's simple. Once again, I am trying to control my world, and it isn't working. I am angry all the time, but I am not ready to leave the marriage. I feel bitter, exhausted, and alone. When my anger subsides, I remember the freedom in letting go. I want to believe that my sense of self-worth is greater than a specific set of circumstances. I decide to give this new idea a try, which requires me to trust myself more deeply than before. I remind myself that no matter what, I am going to be okay.

Wrap-Up: Set Your Prayers Up for Success (No Matter Who or What They Are To)

The second part of Step Eleven—praying only for knowledge of His will for us and the power to carry that out—is critical. It is tempting to pray for the outcomes we so desperately long for, like the health of our sick loved ones, the job promotion, and the safety of our children. The danger in this type of prayer is that it is contingent on a God that can control outcomes. The problem, though, is that life will inevitably throw a curveball that has a devastating outcome. Praying to a God of your own understanding for the things you want is futile, and it has control written all over it. You essentially set yourself up to fail. When one of those things doesn't happen, you collect evidence that there is no God, and you rely once again on your hardwiring when in fear and doubt.

In Twelve Step programs, there is something known as the Eleventh Step Prayer, and it goes like this:

Lord, grant that I may seek rather to comfort, than to be comforted; to understand, than to be understood; to love, than to be loved. For it is by self-forgetting, that one finds. It is by forgiving, that one is forgiven. It is by dying, that one awakens to Eternal Life. Amen.

I know it sounds awfully religious. By now, I hope you've dismantled any beliefs that make the words God, Lord, or anything of its kind unpalatable. But just in case, let's reframe it. What this prayer is essentially saying is that rather than ask for your own needs and desires to be met, just for today you can simply ask to be the best version of yourself. From there, you can pay attention to what shows up. You can imagine a world in which the possibilities are much greater than anything you've thought of yourself. And if it all feels impossible, try this: *Dear universe, show me the way.*

STEP ELEVEN: YOUR VERSION

To hold yourself accountable, set aside a few minutes at the start or end of your day to say a prayer that resonates with you and meditate on the visions that prayer conjures up. Remember that the step begins with the word "sought": "Sought through prayer and meditation to improve our conscious contact with God as we understood Him, praying only for knowledge of His will for us and the power to carry that out."[22] The most important thing about this step is the act of seeking.

When we hit the wall, we seek. When we fall down, we seek. When we are in despair, we seek. We ask for help, we pray to a power greater than ourselves, and we imagine what our highest

---

22 Alcoholics Anonymous World Services, *Twelve Steps and Twelve Traditions*, 96.

self would do. We make space for love and healing. We rest and we dream. We consider what our childlike selves would do and what our most loving friends might say. We sit in the massive discomfort life is throwing at us and we gather strength from the here and now, moment to moment. We pray for access to a power that is uniquely our own—the way we live and love and show up in the world.

I am a big proponent of meditation in many forms: lying down, sitting, standing, walking, or driving. Once you practice seeking conscious contact with a higher power, you realize that it is accessible to you in every moment. You realize that God is everywhere.

A small, sustainable practice is a great start. Maybe you commit to one minute of prayer and meditation a day for three days. Sometimes you can only find a moment to spare, whether it's in traffic on the way to a job interview or in a bathroom stall on a shitty day at work. Something is better than nothing. Wherever you go, no matter what is happening, Step Eleven is available to you. All you can do is try to make conscious contact with a power you believe in, take a deep breath, and keep on keeping on.

12

DEAR JESSICA

SOMETHING VERY SPECIAL HAPPENS WHEN you reach Step Twelve. You wake up each day swelling with pride, knowing you have survived hard things. You have a sense of integrity that comes from being forced to confront the truth and feel it all. You have a new blueprint for living that gives you access to real power—the kind of power you feel when you are armed with self-worth, dignity, and respect. Like many of the other steps, it has two parts: one that requires us to keep practicing new behavior and another that asks us to give back. It goes like this:

> Having had a spiritual awakening as a result of these
> steps, we tried to carry this message to others, and
> to practice these principles in all our affairs.[23]

A spiritual awakening does not necessarily mean a white-light experience or a sense of profound change that hits you like a lightning bolt. Often, spiritual transformation happens slowly

---

23 Alcoholics Anonymous World Services, *Twelve Steps and Twelve Traditions* (New York: Alcoholics Anonymous World Services, 1981), 106.

from thousands of small decisions that move the needle of your life in a new direction. The truth is, even if you are a tiny bit farther along the spiritual path than someone else, you have had a spiritual awakening of sorts. From there, when someone is ready, Step Twelve calls on you to extend your hand and pull them up from the shipwreck. Not so that you drown yourself, but so that your heartbreak is not in vain. So that you take your pain and do something meaningful with it. The final part is about practice. Surprise, surprise.

In a family full of addicts, enablers, and mental illness, I have been tempted to push the program on people many times (and guilty of doing so). I begged Ryan, my mother, my father, and my sister to work the Steps. I was so used to putting the attention outside of myself that it felt like second nature. But once again, I learned the hard way that no one wants unsolicited advice shoved down their throat. In fact, most people just want to be seen and heard. And hardest of all, most people need to hit their own bottom to find the willingness to change.

After trying so hard and so often to save the people I love and failing, I learned how to grieve. I also learned how to go on living, becoming a real-life example of what sobriety looks like. I tried to remind myself that my big, beautiful life was proof that recovery works, and to stay open to the possibility that the people I love might one day become ready to make a start.

THE TRAIL OF TRAGEDY

It was a beautiful, sunny morning on Catalina Island. Now years into a much healthier relationship, my husband and I planned a lovely weekend getaway to this magical place, renting a house near the ocean. The day after we arrived there, our two-year-old, Charly, had woken up terribly early, so I was exhausted when my phone began to ring incessantly. It was my sister, and I had no desire to pick up. As usual, she was clueless about the fact that it was three hours earlier for me, or maybe she didn't care. I hit the red button to end the call. And then it rang again. End call. When it rang a third time, I thought my mother was dead, so I picked up.

"You have to help me." My sister's voice quivered with paranoia and fear. "Someone is in my house."

"What do you mean?!" I said, sitting straight up in bed.

I felt a familiar sinking in my belly. Through quick and shallow breaths, I tried to discern if she was in real or imagined danger. After a couple of minutes, and after she told me her finger was broken and that the person who broke it was in her house, I realized she was high, delusional, and terrified. I woke Ryan up and told him to take the kids outside so I could stay on the phone with my sister. Then I texted Beth, my longtime and now sober friend (the one who came over the night of my overdose), and asked that she be on standby when my sister "came to" to make sure she didn't hurt herself or someone else.

Even in a drugged-up state, my sister knew to call me. She slowly became more lucid and realized that no one was there. She had been high on GHB—otherwise known as "the date rape drug"—a clear liquid that when taken in small amounts makes you feel euphoric, but, in slightly larger amounts, renders you unconscious or dead. She stared at her crooked finger and became frightened that a thing like this could happen to her without any memory of it. I told her Beth was coming over—she happened to live ten minutes away—and I shot it straight.

"If you use again, you're going to die."

We both knew she had been given too many chances, had awoken out of so many blackouts we couldn't keep count. To use again was beyond dangerous. To use again was to commit suicide. Beth arrived, and together, as I sat on the phone, we begged Jessica to go to rehab, an inpatient facility, or any place where the sole focus was on her recovery. But as it often goes, shame held her back. She refused outside help, worried her law license might be threatened, and swore she would go to meetings. That this time it would be different. I held a tiny bit of hope in my heart, despite what I'd witnessed before and despite the statistics being grossly out of her favor.

She did start to go to meetings and got a sponsor, which was such a relief. For a few months, I felt like my sister came back from the dead. Like a sick newcomer, she called me relentlessly in the early days, talking only of herself and her big giant feelings. As I juggled motherhood, business ownership, and marriage, I took her calls because it felt like she was reaching her hand out and I didn't want to miss it. She was finally sober, and I would fit that into my very busy life because I didn't know how long it would last. She would call me on FaceTime, a Red Bull in hand, describing her most recent revelations.

"I've been self-sabotaging for so long because I have no self-worth," she'd say.

"I know. I really do. I promise it gets better," I'd whisper.

These conversations were beautiful. After so much loss, it felt like I got back the sister I loved and missed terribly. Before this, when her addiction had a viselike hold over her, our conversations grazed the surface, and things were always "fine" in her world, an obvious mask to try and keep up appearances. She always said the same thing: the kids were great, work was busy, and her marriage was good enough. Now, early in sobriety and emotionally raw, she was honest. Her kids were the center of her world, but work sucked, she hated herself, and her husband was an asshole.

As she revealed these negative truths about her life, snot dripping down her nose, she seemed different in the best way. Her eyes were brighter. Her voice was hopeful. Her laugh was fast and loud, the way it was when we were kids. All the shit she had piled on top of her broken heart was bubbling to the surface, and she didn't know what to do with it. For me, it felt like a breath of fresh air, a brand-new start to our relationship.

No matter how exhausting her phone calls were, I took them. I was relieved to have her back. I believed unequivocally that she was right where she needed to be. She could now begin to heal from long-term childhood trauma and decades of drug addiction. When my phone rang, I sat quietly on the other end and listened to her unburden her dizzying mind and wounded spirit. Then, I would find a moment to honor her feelings and share my experience.

After those early months, the calls became less frequent. I was worried. Was she healing or relapsing? Something had changed. I could feel a wall go up. When I tried to follow up with her, instead of answering in-depth, she would respond with a simple text about how well she was doing, talking about all her new job opportunities as a lawyer and how she might someday start her own firm.

She was an incredibly high-functioning addict, as so many of us are, and it's part of what kept her sick. She did not just hold down a job, she was promoted time and again because she was so goddamn smart. To the outside world, it seemed as though she was thriving in her personal and professional life. She bought fancy clothes, drove fancy cars, and lived in a fancy part of New Jersey with her husband and two beautiful children.

I became less convinced over those months that she was still sober, but she swore up and down that she was, so I stood back from a distance and gave her room to find her way. I knew from my own recovery and everything I had witnessed at meetings that I couldn't fix or save her. I knew I wasn't her higher power. Instead, I did the only thing I could: I modeled how to live life sober one day at a time, acting as an anchor of stability for my sister through actions rather than words.

For the next six months, we spoke intermittently, and I wondered again and again if she had relapsed. She would text here and there about how many months sober she was and ask, "Aren't you proud of me Sammy?" I struggled to say yes because her distance felt all too familiar. It's the kind of distance addicts put between themselves and their loved ones so they're not found out. I knew from personal experience.

"Of course I am," I would write back, nonetheless.

I kept trying to trust her. She wasn't contacting me much, other than to share that she was getting divorced and that soon she would tell me just how bad the marriage really was. Then, nearly a year after she broke that finger, I received some of the most harrowing pictures I have ever seen. They were pictures of my sister's face, bludgeoned and bruised. She had two black eyes, a broken nose, a split lip, and a cracked tooth. She sent five or six of these shocking photographs with a sarcastic message underneath: "Courtesy of slips, trips, and falls."

I called in a panic.

"Oh my God, Jess!" I shouted into the phone. "What the fuck happened?"

She told me a tale about holding groceries in both hands, slipping, and breaking her nose.

"You won't believe this, but a few days after that fall, I slipped in the tub, split my lip, and cracked my tooth! My boyfriend is so amazing, he has been helping so much. I'm definitely getting a nose job once the swelling goes down, and he's going to pay for it. Isn't that so sweet?"

I listened silently, knowing she was lying straight through those teeth.

"You never told me you had a boyfriend," I said. "Did he do this to you, Jess?"

"Oh my God, no! He is the nicest man I have ever met. He would never hurt me!" she swore.

"Did you relapse?" I asked calmly.

"Sam," she said, "if there was any person on earth I could talk to about a relapse, it's you—you understand addiction and would never judge me. I know what this looks like, but I swear I'm fine."

"All right," I said, shaking my head, "but just so you know, this is not how we are going to build back a relationship after so much trust has been broken. From now on, it is not okay to call me every day and then disappear, only to reappear with horrific photos that would have knocked a total stranger on their ass, let alone your own sister. If we're going to reestablish trust, then you have to consistently be there in the good times and the bad and not just call me in crisis."

She was stunned by my honesty and then quietly agreed. When we hung up, the fixer and saver inside of me was wildly activated. The swirls of energy in my nervous system made me want to call her back and beg her to be honest. The terror of losing her made me want to slap her sober and force her into rehab. I had already lost Charlie, and I didn't want to bury my own sister.

I held space for my broken heart and took a long, deep breath. I watched the hardwired parts of me rev up until they settled, and then I practiced my new behaviors. I paused. I prayed. I called my sober girlfriends and asked for help.

"My sister sent me some awful pictures and it's just too heavy to hold on my own. Can you help me carry it?" We all agreed that the photos seemed like proof that my sister was using again, and we said a group prayer that she would get the help she needed sooner rather than later. Then her friends started calling and sending me messages.

"Sam, hi, this is Victoria. I'm not sure if you've seen your sister's face but I'm really worried about her. Please call me back," she said. She was a friend Jess had used drugs with over the years. I didn't like or trust her one bit.

On Instagram, another friend I had never met messaged me: "Hi Sam, my name is Tracy. I am your sister's hairstylist. I'm not sure if you've seen her face, but we need to talk. Call me right away."

I called her, hoping she had more information. She didn't.

"What can we do? We have to help her!" she cried.

I exhaled.

"My sister is very sick," I said. "She knows she is an addict, and she is swearing up and down that she's sober. I have said and done all that I can do for more than ten years, and we are absolutely powerless over her addiction."

Tracy said nothing, and after a few moments, I heard her crying faintly.

I knew there was only so much I could do to help my sister after all this time. But that night, the sting of a guilty conscience shot me out of bed. *What if I could do more? What if I could say just the right thing this time to make her finally come clean? What if this was her last cry for help?* I had tried to save her so many times before, despite being told again and again that only the addict can save herself.

But like all the people who love the addict, I kept trying to reimagine how this time it might be different. I could fly back East, take her to rehab, and help her get sober. I could show her the desperation in my eyes for the sister I missed so much and wanted back. I could shake her into submission once and for all.

I finally fell asleep, restless and distressed. That night was filled with scary dreams. In one, she and I spoke sweetly about our lives. She looked so beautiful, her green eyes and pale skin glowing without the caked-on foundation and penciled-in eyebrows. Then, suddenly, I stopped and shouted, "But you wouldn't know any of this because you're dead!"

I woke up in a sweat and decided to call her after my morning coffee. Rather than turn away from the sickness, I turned toward it in the only way I could. Instead of accusing and judging, I offered and extended. One more time, I reached out my hand, trying to pull her out of her misery without hurting myself. Between the new boyfriend and the history of addiction, I didn't know if she was being beaten up, blacking out, or a nasty combination of both. I asked her to tell me the truth.

"I know how this looks," she said, "but I swear it was just a string of bad luck."

She clung to her story. In hindsight, this is exceptionally sad because it shines a light on the magnitude of her shame. She was so sick inside, so ashamed of who she was, that lying to her sister was easier than facing her demons.

Weeks later, Ryan and I flew to Austin for the weekend to look for an investment property, stopping in cafes, wandering around new neighborhoods, and resting at night in a boutique inn just outside the city. It was the longest we had been away without our kids since they were born, and it was spectacular. We explored new places, laughed a lot, and felt a surge of possibility for our future.

After spending the morning in San Antonio, we drove back to the airport, excited to see the kids but sad to end our precious time together. Happy and relaxed, we played Candy Crush on our phones and waited for boarding to begin. My phone started buzzing.

It was an area code I didn't recognize, so at first I ignored it, blaming spam for the thousandth time. But then it buzzed a second time. And a third. Then, I received a text from the same number: "Sam, it's Victoria. Please call me right away." Any call from Victoria felt dangerous. My heart started pounding.

Please, God, no. No, no, no.

I called her right away, barely able to dial the numbers with my shaking hands, adrenaline coursing through my body.

"Victoria, what is it?" I said. "Please tell me it's not about my sister."

"I'm so sorry, Sam," she whispered. "She passed."

I erupted into shrieking sobs—a wailing so primal that it ravages your insides. As I clenched my eyes and collapsed on the ground, I had an out-of-body experience, watching the neural pathways that connected me to my sister sear and die. Impossible grief. Guttural pain. A paralysis of fear that reminded me of the call about my father. A loss of a part of me, the acute death of all my hopes and dreams for the sister I would never have again, sober or not.

My sobs were disruptive and out of place at the airport, and my husband held me tight, suggesting that I skip the flight back to LA and get on a plane to New Jersey instead. The thought of being alone in that moment was nightmarish, so I wiped my eyes and tilted down the wide brim of my hat.

"No!" I shouted. "Get me on the plane."

Ryan ushered me down the long aisle lined with passengers having apparently normal days and I wondered how I was going to survive this disaster. This moment, which I had imagined and dreaded many times, had actually come to pass. The worst-case scenario had happened. And somehow, I had to put one foot in front of the other, fly home to my sweet children, and tell them, "Mommy is really sad." Then, I had to function in a way that no one should have to right after a huge loss—I booked a flight, packed a bag, and got on the first plane to New Jersey the next morning.

The next week of my life was unimaginable. Not only did I break the news to my sister's ex-husband, but I also broke the news to my mother. When I called Beth sobbing, letting her know what had happened and asking if I could stay with her, she welcomed me with open arms. She saved my soul then the same way she had saved my life a decade earlier in my New York City apartment. She fed me, held me, and walked straight into the pain with me. When I finally showed up at her door, I dropped to the ground. She held me until I couldn't stay awake anymore, drained from traveling and depressed beyond measure. The next morning, we began searching for my sister's will, which Victoria swore Jessica had hidden among the rest of her important paperwork.

My sister's landlord met with me and offered awkward condolences. She handed me the key, warning me that Benny, my sister's ex-husband, might want to come by and that he wasn't welcome. No longer able to protect my sister, I was ready to protect her things at all costs. I didn't know much, but I knew she felt serious rage and resentment toward her ex. During the months leading up to her death, she painted an ugly picture of him: He taunted her appearance, refused to pay alimony, and wanted sole custody of the kids.

My mission was to tear the apartment apart until I found the will. I knew I was the executor, and, helpless as I felt, I found a touch of solace knowing that I could honor her wishes. A detective met me at the house and told me that it appeared Jessica died in her sleep of an overdose but that she had to rule out foul play. As I watched her lips move, I felt like I was a character in a made-for-TV movie, listening to details of my sister's life and death that sent shock waves through my nervous system.

Intellectually, it wasn't surprising that her place was in shambles, a seemingly beautiful apartment packed with pretty paintings, new furniture, and expensive equipment that hid the lies and secrets of an addict behind the closet doors. Purses filled with empty GHB bottles. Safes busted open with nothing inside. Stacks of paperwork from years before, checks uncashed, bills unpaid. I would be hunting for paperwork in the very place where she died, tearing through bags and drawers and closets where empty pill bottles lived, and ripping sheets off the blood-stained mattress where she took her last breath.

The smell of her clothes both soothed and disgusted me, a strong floral scent that shot into my nasal passages and lodged there permanently. Emotionally, I was gutted by every item I touched, wondering how many times my big sister went unconscious in this shirt or those pants, how many sprays of perfume she used to cover up her sorrow and how many tears she never released because they scared her too much. I rummaged and ripped through her drawers, cabinets, and closets, stopping at intervals to walk outside and scream.

My mother came and sat with me through those awful days, distant and despondent. I threw items across the living room, and she sat there, motionless. The caretaker, again, in this awful tragedy. When Jess's ex called, I screamed at him, telling him that my sister hated him and he had to leave me alone. As those first forty-eight hours wore on, I grew crazed with rage.

The closest lead I had to unearthing her will was to an estate attorney whose paperwork was in the basement. When I called, he said Jessica had started to write her will with him a few years ago and made a draft making me the executor. But she never came back to sign it or notarize it, so it was null and void. I collapsed on the dirty basement floor amid stacks of legal documents and cried.

I surrendered. I could either go insane trying to do this alone, carrying my sister's hate for her ex in my heart, or I could call Benny, who was also the sole guardian of my niece and nephew, and tell him I needed help. As my eyes glazed over with tears, I stumbled on their wedding photo. Once upon a time, he and my sister were happily married, and I called him brother. All at once, I considered what he must have endured being married to and then divorced from an addict. I had spent years listening to my sister's side, but in the meantime, he had been raising those kids with a very sick and unreliable partner. That must have been torture. When I couldn't stand being in that apartment any longer, I got in my car and called him.

He picked up, his voice thick. "Sam."

"I can't do this by myself," I said. "I'm sorry I got so angry, but I don't know what's what anymore. I'm so devastated. I need your help."

Benny was kind and gracious. A wave of relief came over me, and the next day, he and his family members drove up to the apartment in a giant U-Haul truck. Doing the only thing we had control over, each person moved quickly into action, sifting through my sister's things, keeping what seemed important and tossing the rest. An impossible task. Benny looked older and haggard, with dark circles under his eyes and thinned brown hair. I could tell instantly that my sister's death had taken a toll on him. The moment our eyes met, we rushed toward and collapsed against one another, sobbing, gripping each other's waists as if to beg the other to never leave. Regardless of my personal feelings, he might have been the only person who knew my sister as well as I did.

My niece and nephew, Kloe and Wyatt, came running over.

"Hi, Aunt Sammy!" They smiled. "How are you?"

Their cheerful and inquisitive nature was haunting—they seemed oddly unfazed by what brought us together. Benny's fiancée, Ivanna, came to the house too, and gave me a big hug.

"I'm so sorry," she whispered.

My mom and I shot wide-eyed glances at one another, stunned at the view inside our extended family's life, one that we did not know. When someone you love is an addict, it's not just their own life that is hidden. It is everything that extends tangentially from their life too. It had been years since we'd had any real connection to these kids and to what they'd gone through. As they sifted through my sister's belongings, they kept looking at Ivanna and saying things like, "Mom, do you think I should keep this?"

My heart both ached and acknowledged a hard truth. My sister had been gone for so long, falling unconscious in the presence of her children, throwing them across the room in blackouts, and abandoning them in drug hazes so many times, that child protective services knew them well. All the while, in her place, another woman had been showing up consistently, loving them and nurturing them to the point that they called her "Mom." It was both beautiful and excruciating.

We packed and we worked together. I kissed and squeezed my sister's children, an attempt to feel connected to the once warm skin of my sister. I smelled their heads and tried to memorize the scent, an attempt to replace the ghostly stench of Jessica's perfume. In the darkness of my sister's death, I held on tightly to the light in my niece's and nephew's eyes.

A detective who had visited my sister's house many times filled me in on some details. The new boyfriend had been ruled out for foul play, the autopsy was underway, and the black eye and broken nose were from a blackout when Jessica did too much GHB. Her boyfriend stopped by one evening and found the door locked but heard water coming down the pipes. He immediately panicked and climbed through an open window to find her submerged in her bathtub, drowning and unconscious from an overdose. He pulled her out and pumped her stomach until she woke up. He begged her to go to the hospital, so she did, and then she came back home and kept on using—because that's what addicts do.

I wondered how I would go on with the knowledge that, as I witnessed those horrific pictures, as I called and tried to bring her back to me, she was alone in her misery, drowning in shame and sorrow in her tub. How would I go on living with the image of my sister underwater and underground?

And yet death forces you to suit up and show up, clean out dirty apartments, and plan "celebration of life" parties. It forces you to go through decades of photographs and friendships and contact people and family and break the terrible news again and again. It forces you to either run away from yourself or become the most connected to yourself you've ever been. It is the wildest, most out-of-control experience I know, and I felt like I was walking on the earth raw and untethered. Everything that hurt was excruciating, and everything that felt good made me want to explode with joy.

I found a place near her apartment that would take her body, prepare it for viewing, and then cremate it. It seemed good enough and, in my haste to perform all my duties as quickly as possible so I could get back home and grieve, I set things up without doing much research. Days into packing up and rummaging through my sister's belongings, it was time to go to the funeral home to view the body and pay for her remains. My mother came with me, and Beth was on her way.

As we pulled up, the place looked less like a funeral parlor and more like a dilapidated house. I had a terrible feeling, the eerie facility magnifying the tragic circumstances. My mother and I exchanged wary glances as we walked to the door, and the manager pulled into the driveway. He let us in. It was dark and dusty, with lines of folding chairs and walkers against the wall and a makeshift, church-style seating area. It reminded me of an old, dirty church that held round-the-clock AA meetings. A smoke alarm chirped, low on battery, and the sound pierced my eardrums. I felt spooked as he invited us into what looked like the main office. My understanding was that we would pay first and then have a moment before we viewed my sister's remains.

Without warning, my mother and I were confronted with Jessica's body, stuffed in a cardboard box. I screamed and gripped my mouth with horror. Her face was glossy and wet, her skin was bruised, her hair thinned, and her expression sad. I remembered my dad's body being well presented, cared for, colorful and dry, so I could rest my cheek against his. But my sister was wet and pale and cold. Her arms were hidden, and her lips pointed down. There was nowhere to touch her, to latch on to her physical form one last time. It was unbearable.

I ran out of the room and out of the house and into the sunlight and wept. Beth showed up moments later and was kind enough to go in and take over. Another beautiful moment inside one of the worst times of my life—the way she helped us, the way she went in and out of that awful place to check on me and my mother until we were done. When she sat on the front porch with me, I rested the side of my head on her shoulder and cried, wiping snot on my sleeve and staring up at the perfectly blue sky.

The next day was the celebration of life. I littered the restaurant we'd chosen with flowers and pictures and wore something nice with my sister's jewelry hugging my neck. I wrapped myself around old friends and cried on shoulders and saw hope shattered in people's eyes. Benny said the kids wanted to perform for their mother— Wyatt, eleven, would play the violin and Kloe, nine, would sing.

Wyatt wore a blue button-down and khaki pants and carried his violin to the front of the room. He looked around warily and then propped the instrument on his left shoulder and began. The melody was slow and beautiful, and the onlookers had watery eyes. Everyone clapped when he finished, and he smiled as he sat back down. When it was Kloe's turn, she stood up and crossed over to Ivanna for words of encouragement. Then, she walked to the front of the room, turned back around, and rushed to Benny, letting out a giant sob on his chest. She was a spitting image of my sister, with her long blonde hair, light eyes, and narrow face. I wanted her to run to me. I wanted to hug and squeeze her and tell her she could do this really hard thing, because it would feel like I was telling my sister the same. She looked over at me but didn't move.

After several pep talks and deep breaths, she walked to the front of the room and sang. She cried her way through the entire song, her pitch off and her tone cracked under the weight of her loss. I cried with her and for her, though I had deep relief at the sight of her wet face. There it was. The truth. The love and grief for her dead mother, gushing out. Everyone cried together in this profound moment of sorrow. The party came and went, the pictures got pulled off the wall, and the flowers got taken to different people's homes. And just like that, my sister's life was over.

As people returned to their everyday lives, I wondered how I would use the tools of recovery to navigate this great loss. Was my sobriety strong enough to keep me from a relapse? This was one of the contingencies of my sobriety. I can stay sober *if and only if* my sister doesn't die of a drug overdose. Otherwise, all bets were off.

I was standing on the precipice of either diving further into my recovery or falling back into the old faulty wiring of substance abuse, a guaranteed death sentence should I want that. I thought about all the sober women who had lost people they loved. My sponsor lost both her husbands to cancer, and she was thirty-four years sober. She seemed happy and full of life. I thought about what I had overcome in my childhood, in my marriage, and in my recovery up until this point. I knew that to drink was to die, and I decided I wanted to fully live.

I flew home and felt a deep wave of relief when I set foot on the California soil. Here, in this place, I had built a big, beautiful life, with evidence all around me of what my sobriety had given me. I had worked hard to get here. And yet, the big house, the strong marriage, and the healthy kids were all tinged with deep sorrow, a constant reminder of the life my sister couldn't find and wouldn't know. We had been two people in the same house, with the same upbringing and same predisposition for addiction, both in many ways hardwired and then unwired the same way. But the ending, the rewiring, was different. One had bottomed out and then built a better life; the other was taken out until there was nothing left but ashes and heartache.

As I drove through the streets toward my home, I wondered if I would ever feel joyful again. But then I remembered that because grief hurts like hell, and it was here to stay, I needed to chase down joy like it's my birthright, because it is. Spiritually speaking, joy is as essential as the air we breathe—a dire necessity if we want to keep hope alive.

After her death, I felt shackles from my wrists and ankles fall to the ground. The running narrative that I had to "be some-body" to write a book, have a "certain amount of followers" to start a podcast, or "keep daydreaming" if I wanted to switch careers had finally collapsed. Once and for all, I said fuck it. I didn't know where I was going or who I was becoming, but I knew I needed to do the kind of work in the world that reflected the things I had lived through. I knew I had to tell the truth about my life and help others. I knew I had to integrate the years of clinical work with the years of recovery. If there is such a thing as a silver lining, the gift of my sister's death is that it gave me permission to fully live.

AN ALTERNATE LOOK AT STEP TWELVE

As I write this, my mother is once again in an acute manic episode. After Jessica's death, she fell into a deep depression and isolated herself in her room during the long winter days in New York. I checked on her often and I understood her pain. Eight months later, she told me the facility she lived in was being sold and she was moving to California.

The relief I felt at having the one remaining family member close by is hard to explain. I had buried my father and my sister, taking lonely plane rides and scattering ashes around different parts of the city until I felt like there was nothing left of me. Imagining that any health issue my mother might face would fall entirely in my lap when I lived three thousand miles away sounded like another living nightmare. At the very least, even if she went insane, I would be nearby. I would have the immediate support of my friends and family. I would not feel so utterly alone.

Six months into her move, I got the opportunity of a lifetime. By chance, I met a recording artist in a dance class I taught at the local Equinox near my house. After a chat over coffee and an aggressive showcasing of my work, he hired me as a choreographer and asked me to join him on a five-city tour in Japan. My childhood dreams were materializing right before my eyes. At forty years old, married with two kids, I was called to do the thing I had always wanted to do. Call it divine intervention, a God shot, a miracle, or when hard fucking work meets great timing. I jumped at the chance, and I had the time of my life.

Halfway through, though, my mother's text messages had an eerie familiarity. Racing thoughts, grand delusions, excessive spending. *Fuck.* I called Ryan to ask if my mother's behavior seemed off. He didn't want to stress me out, but he admitted that she seemed manic. Though I felt a familiar pit of despair, I had enough recovery to recognize my powerlessness over it all—and the last thing I was going to do was ruin my trip. Instead, I surrendered control and danced my heart out. I knew I would come home to a mess, so in the meantime, I played and played to my heart's content.

Once I got back, it was painfully clear that she was manic. Eventually, she admitted to cutting her medication in half. I felt anxiety and fear balloon inside of me as I contemplated what to say and do.

I weighed my options.

Reaction 1: Pushing (Not Carrying) the Message

I pick her up from her apartment and look her squarely in the eye and say, "Mom, you're acting manic. This has happened many times before and it never ends well. You need to get back on your meds before you end up in a hospital."

She looks at me, outraged. For the next several minutes she goes on a tirade, telling me how happy she is and how great she feels and *why can't I just let her be happy.* She tells me that Jessica tried to ruin her life and now I was doing the same. The more she shouts, the louder I yell: "*Stop screaming at me! I will not be emotionally abused by you anymore! Do you hear me?*"

She screams louder, and I drive her back home, unlock the doors, and watch her slam the passenger-side door. I drop my head in my hands and sob.

Reaction 2: The Power of Practice

I take note of her behavior and, coupled with her admission to cutting her meds in half, decide to wait until later to address it. I recognize my powerlessness over her mental illness and know that if I try to control it, I will end up feeling insane. I turn inward and ask my higher power for guidance. I wait several hours and send her a message:

> Mom, I've thought about what you told me, and I'm worried about you. In the past, when you've stopped your meds, you become manic and end up hospitalized. I'm wondering if it makes more sense to make an appointment with a psychiatrist and figure out the best course of action. I love you and I love how close we are. I don't want that to change. What do you think of that idea?

To my surprise, she agrees. Despite many other irrational requests and behaviors (for which I have to set massive boundaries), I take her to see the doctor because it is the only way I feel I can give back without hurting myself in the process.

Wrap-Up: It's Lifelong Work

I picked up every tool I could from recovery and therapy to navigate this very difficult situation. Fun fact: Despite the intervention and a plan for titrating her meds upward, she is still currently manic. And I am still, to the best of my ability, trying to practice these principles in all my affairs. Some days it's easier than others.

There is a reason why addicts stay in Twelve Step programs

for their entire lives. No matter how many situations we navigate, there will inevitably be a new one. Maybe we have lost a pet but not a parent. Maybe our best friend has cancer, but we've always been healthy. What happens when we are finally faced with the one thing we can't imagine surviving? We will need help getting through it. We will need love, support, and community. We will need a blueprint for how to survive the heartbreak. And in the dark, when everyone is asleep, we will need a God of our own understanding.

STEP TWELVE: YOUR VERSION

Now it's your turn. As a reminder, Step Twelve is "Having had a spiritual awakening as the result of these steps, we tried to carry this message to alcoholics, and to practice these principles in all our affairs."[24]

If you have done the work up until this point, then you are more prepared than you realize. Here we go.

1. Think of at least one hard thing you have worked through.
2. Consider how you might use the experience to help someone else who is struggling with the same thing. It can go something like this: "I have some experience around that. I am happy to share it with you if you think it would help." If they decline, you did your duty. If they accept, all you have to do is speak from your heart.
3. Tell the truth. You will see how that feels when you're done.

Most of the time, when we come from a place of empathy and

24 Alcoholics Anonymous World Services, *Twelve Steps and Twelve Traditions*, 106.

understanding, there is a beautiful exchange that results in more love, connection, and meaning in our lives. It often answers the question, "Why did this happen to me?" And if not, it just feels good to help people. The next part is more of an "every twenty-four hours" thing. It doesn't have to be overwhelming; it can just be practical.

No matter what happens in your life, you can draw from the Twelve Steps and apply them to the current situation. That is how you practice. That is how old patterns morph into new ones. That is how a life riddled with chaos and dysfunction becomes a life filled with joy and connection.

If I can do it, so can you.

CONCLUSION

THIS BOOK IS THE CULMINATION of everything I have learned in my life up until this point. It is the raw, honest tale of a life without the Twelve Steps versus a life with them. The truth is, every twenty-four hours I need any one of these steps so that I can navigate life with more inner peace. On a good day, the main thing I am powerless over is the traffic, I'm aligned with my higher power, have no amends to make, and am kind and compassionate to myself and others. On a bad day, I have to remember I am powerless over my mother's mental illness and my sister's overdose, that God isn't working against me, that in my desire to be loved I can have unrealistic expectations of my friends and family, and that when I am stuck in self-will, I am unable to tap into my intuition, disconnected from my higher power and overwhelmed with emotion.

Fortunately (and unfortunately), we never graduate from the school of life. Our spiritual curriculum continues to evolve and deepen, and we either turn toward the pain and learn something or we numb it. Remember when I told you my mother is, in real time, acutely manic? Guess what. This level of despair is forcing me, yet again, into more Twelve Step work. This time around, I am focusing on my inner child, learning how to reparent myself, regulate my nervous system, and build secure attachments.

Despite all the work I have done, this new spiritual crisis has revealed a layer of trauma that is begging to be healed—one that forces me to reckon with the integration of my head and heart when it comes to interpersonal relationships. I see now that some of my friendships were built on a cracked foundation—one where I believed that if I loved the person hard enough, they would never leave me.

The deep nuance of this core belief means that my nervous system is so comfortable over-giving and over-sharing to feel safe, worthy, and loved that it continues to repeat those patterns into adulthood. What happens is the very opposite of what I'm longing for. I cannot control the other person, I become anxiously attached, I beg for breadcrumbs, and ultimately, they leave (just like I thought they would). The work, then, is deep and difficult. It requires me to face my grief head-on and implement the Steps around issues that stem back from childhood trauma.

It looks something like this: I am powerless over my mother's mental illness, and when I abandon myself to care for her my life becomes unmanageable. Without a grounded perspective, I lose mental clarity around how to take care of myself. I become fearful and exhausted. The current work, then, requires me to learn and practice a new idea of safety—when my eight-year-old self becomes dysregulated, I ask her what she needs. I practice gentle actions to calm myself down: deep breathing, meditation, yoga, or simply a hand on my heart.

After so much loss, I am truly interested in the business of living. I have seen firsthand what happens to people who shut down and numb out in the presence of pain. They live with armor around their heart, self-righteous indignation, and a kind of self-pity that bypasses any attempt at personal accountability. They blame everything on everyone else and have no real joy or purpose. Or they cover their heartbreak with alcohol, sex, money, clothing, fitness, social media, and drugs until it kills them. I refuse to have a tragic ending. I refuse to continue a cycle of soul sickness.

The story of my life might be riddled with pain and loss, but I hold the pen. I am the author. If I do nothing else right in this life, I know this much is true: I am the cycle breaker. I am changing the trajectory of my ancestral heritage away from mental illness and addiction and toward trauma-informed healing and spiritual evolution. For me, that is everything.

Because inside of me is where love lives, where truth speaks, and where my fire stays lit. So, when I need rest, I sleep; when I need movement, I practice yoga; when I need belly laughter, I text my best friend; when I need soothing, I seek out a loved one capable of offering that comfort. When I need to cry, I let myself sob; and when I need to create, I throw myself into my imagination.

You now have access to the Steps in a way that is relatable regardless of the life situation you're in. Whether you're going through something big or small, these steps are tools in the toolbox that you can pick up whenever you want to help uncover the root cause of the issue and gain access to real power—the kind that lives inside you and is always available. They are the gateway between soul sickness and soul health, a guarded heart and an open one. Simply put, they are the difference between being half dead or fully alive.

When my kids and their kids and their kids read this book, they will know the truth—that life is hard and messy and beautiful and that they can do hard things. That there is forgiveness on the other side of betrayal, recovery on the other side of addiction, and joy on the other side of grief. What a miracle.

For additional resources, please see the websites of the following Twelve Step programs:

- Alcoholics Anonymous: www.aa.org
- Al-Anon Family Groups: www.al-anon.org
- Adult Children of Alcoholics: www.adultchildren.org

APPENDIX

A LETTER TO MY SISTER

Dear Jessica:

They put you in a box. A cold, dirty cardboard box. I walked into the office to take care of payment for your remains, an already unimaginable requirement when you've lost a loved one.

He didn't warn me, though.

I walked in and your body was there. Your skin was glossy. Your hair was wet and wavy and your lips pointed down. You looked so sad.

Your skin had bruises from the recent surgery to fix your face after the fall. The fall I now know happened in a blackout, when you were high and numb and unconscious, so you didn't have to feel anything anymore.

But even your new nose and plump lips and cover-up couldn't hide your hurt. Even in your death, I could see your pain. I'm not angry that you lied, I'm furious that the disease had you strangled and suffocated and submerged. Your friends called and texted and begged to do something, anything, to make your heart stop hurting.

There is nothing for us to do, I reasoned. We just have to love her from far away.

So I called you after the fall and told you that it seemed like there might be more to the story—more than just a tale of slips, trips, and falls—than what you shared.

And I didn't press.

But I said if there is, you're safe to share it with me.

I held space for you, your mistakes, your shame. But like a tidal wave your shame wrapped you up and sloshed you around and made sure to throw you to the bottom again and again. Broken bones, broken heart.

Your shame made you fix your lips and your nose and your chest and your thighs, but it forgot to fix your broken heart. Your shame colored your hair red and bought shoes and clothes and purses and kept thinking that if your outsides were pretty and polished and perfect that no one could see your insides. No one could see that you were a small girl who was forced against her will again and again and who shoved that pain down deep and covered it with cleavage and attention and accolades.

I saw it. And I always saw you underneath. I saw your beautiful heart before someone broke it, your frizzy hair and awkward nose before someone fixed it, and your healthy mind before drugs diseased it.

You gave shame your power. And it put you in a cardboard box.

I couldn't even touch your face.

So I promise to never let shame put a noose around my neck again. It doesn't have a seat at the table, a room in my house, or a resting place in my body. It doesn't get to decide what I deserve. It doesn't tell me to slowly die because I'm not worth living. It doesn't break my nose or break my heart and leave me for dead and then have me coming back for more.

No.

The box you were in was the one shame wanted for you. It was small and dark and cold. But you didn't fit into that box; you were much bigger. I can only try and picture you dancing above it, breaking down walls and boundaries, crushing the armor around your heart once and for all. Being all of who you are and abandoning what shame told you to be. And in that place, we can dance together again. We can swing our hair with reckless abandon until the sun comes up.

ABOUT THE AUTHOR

SAMANTHA BLAKE HARTE is a yoga-certified doctor of physical therapy, performing artist, and podcast host. With more than two decades in the fitness industry and fifteen years of sobriety, Dr. Harte is a living embodiment of her personal and professional experiences. She calls vulnerability her superpower and sees her soul work as the necessary bridge between the life she had and the life she has created.

As a licensed clinician, Dr. Harte is known for her work in functional biomechanics and movement pattern retraining with a passion for injury prevention. After years in recovery, Dr. Harte sees an inextricable connection between the rewiring process of the nervous system in the physical and emotional realms. She also is the host of the weekly Spotify and Apple podcast *The Truth about Addiction*, in which she has raw and honest conversations about addiction, recovery, and the ongoing challenges of living sober. She believes the greatest thing she can do is live and love with her whole heart. She currently resides in Thousand Oaks, California, with her husband and their two amazing kids.